Arthur Ontario
in Colour Photos,
Saving Our History
One Photo at a Time

Photography
by Barbara Raué
2014

Series Name:
Cruising Ontario

Book 82: Arthur

Cover photo: 171 Isabella Street East

Series Name: Cruising Ontario
Saving Our History One Photo at a Time

Other Books by Barbara Raue

Coins of Gold

Arrows, Indians and Love

The Life and Times of Barbara
Volume 1: Inventions That Have Enhanced My Life
Volume 2: Entertainment That I Have Enjoyed
Volume 3: East Coast Trips
Volume 4: Olympics Have Always Intrigued Me
Volume 5: Wonders of the World
Volume 6: Caribbean Cruises We Have Enjoyed
Volume 7: Animals
Volume 8: Storms and Other Major Disasters in My Lifetime
Volume 9: Wars, Terrorist Attacks and Major Disasters

The Cromwell Family Book

Laura Secord Discovered

Visit Barbara's website to view all of her books
http://barbararaue.ca

Arthur

Arthur is located just north of Highway 6 and Wellington Road 109 in the township of Wellington North.

Arthur, named for Arthur Wellesley, Duke of Wellington, was the southern terminus of the Garafraxa "colonization road" to Owen Sound. Settlers arrived in 1840 with the town site being officially surveyed in 1846. The establishment of saw and grist mills hastened growth in the community which was also the natural market centre for the area's agricultural production.

In 1851 a post office was opened and the first church and school were organized. A weekly newspaper, The Arthur Enterprise News, began publication in 1863 and a Division Court met at Arthur. In 1872, a station of the Toronto Grey and Bruce Railway was opened in the community.

In 1897, Arthur was one of the first villages in Ontario to be served by a power transmission line. There were no meters, but people were charged ten cents for each light bulb used. Power was available in the evenings and was cut off at midnight.

James Morrison, an influential activist in farmers' causes, lived two kilometers south of Arthur. He entered politics in the early 1900s, a time when many farmers felt ignored in an increasingly urban and industrial society. Morrison helped form the United Farmers of Ontario (UFO) and the United Farmers' Cooperative in 1914. Morrison advocated cooperative effort among farmers.

Table of Contents

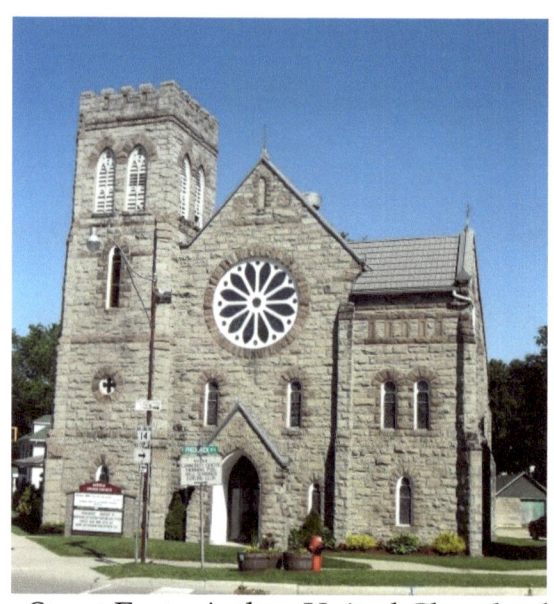

101 Tucker Street East - Arthur United Church – bell tower, rose window

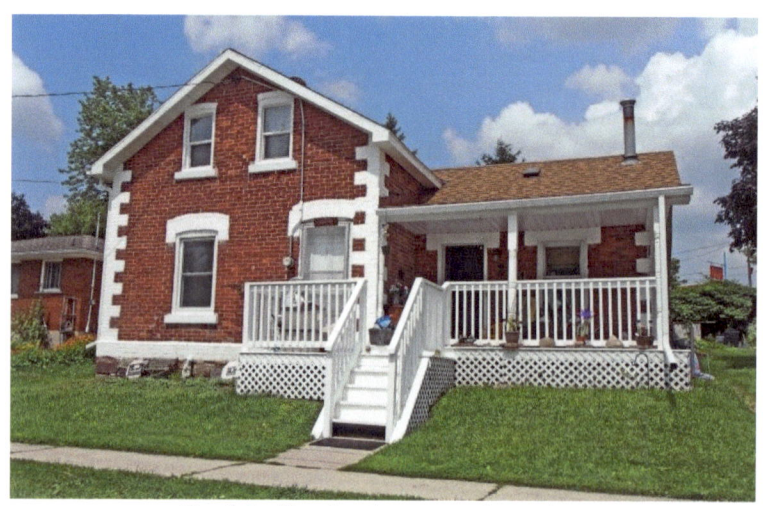

Gothic Revival, corner quoins

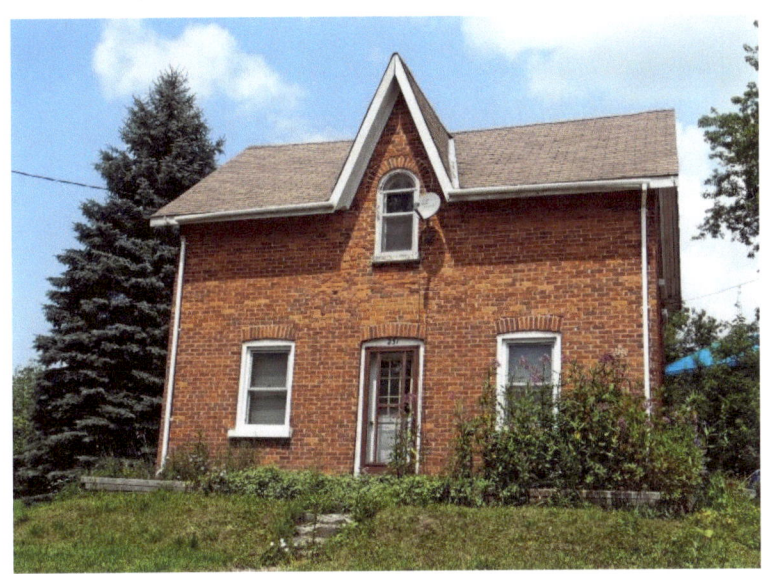

231 Edward Street – Gothic Revival

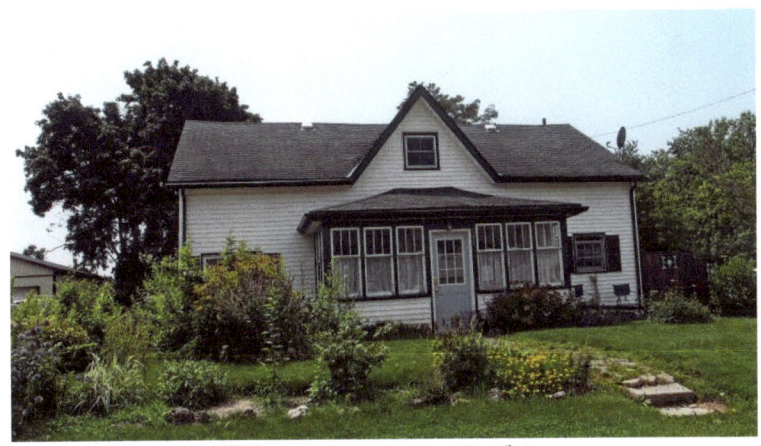

Edward Street – Gothic

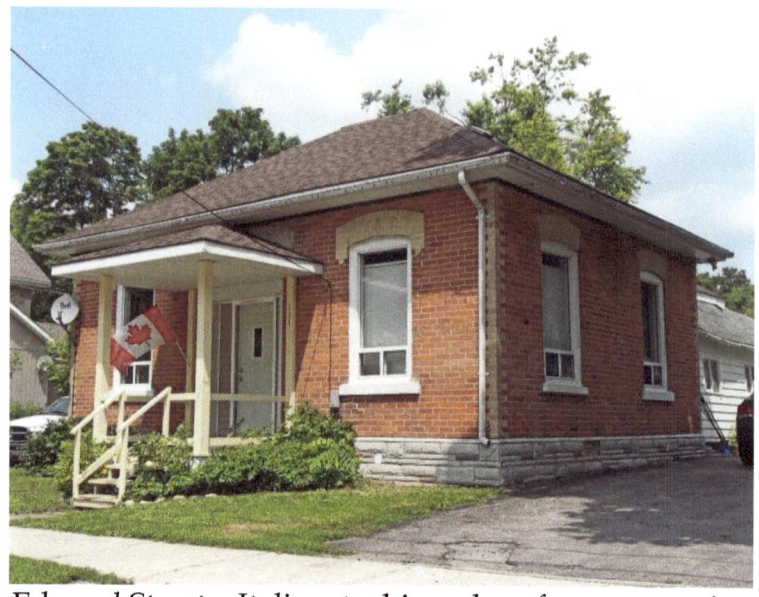

Edward Street – Italianate, hipped roof, corner quoins

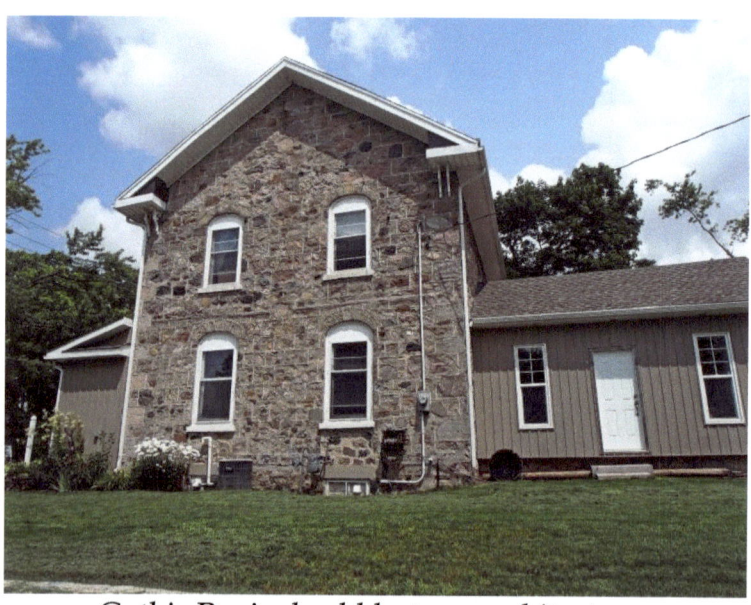

Gothic Revival cobblestone architecture,
cornice return on gable

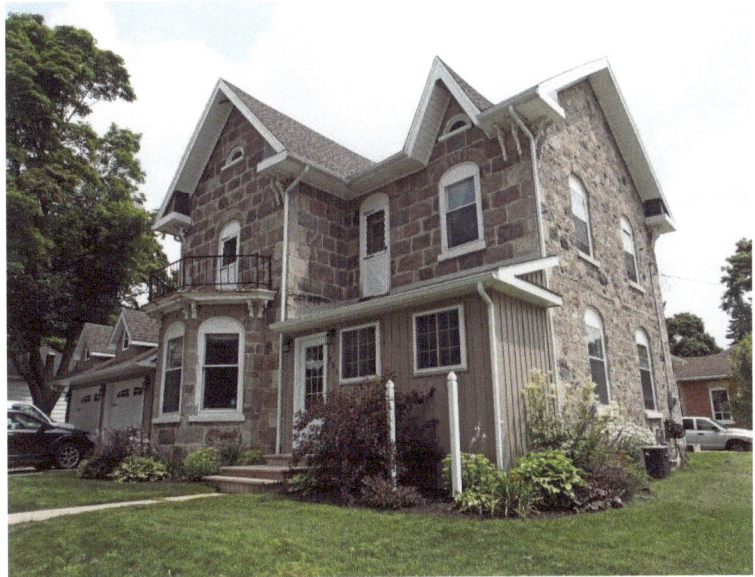

131 Frederick Street West - Gothic Revival, cobblestone architecture, cornice brackets, cornice return on gables

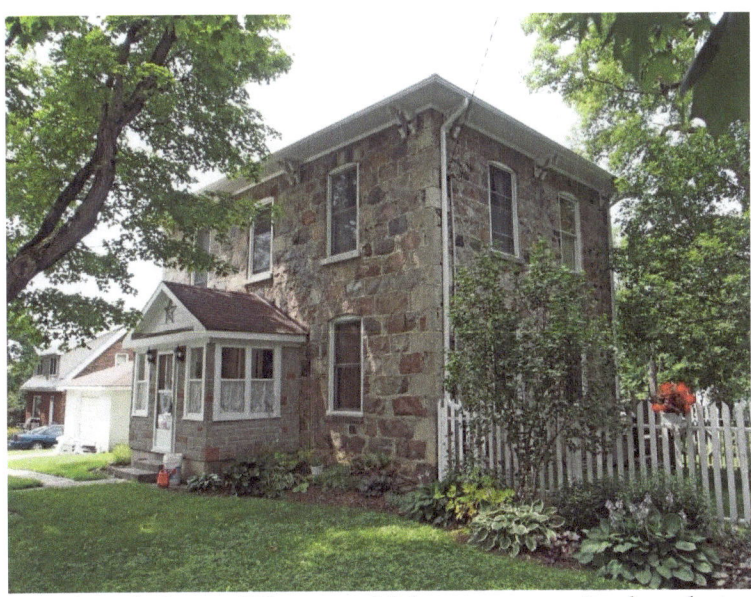

Frederick Street West – cobblestone, cornice brackets

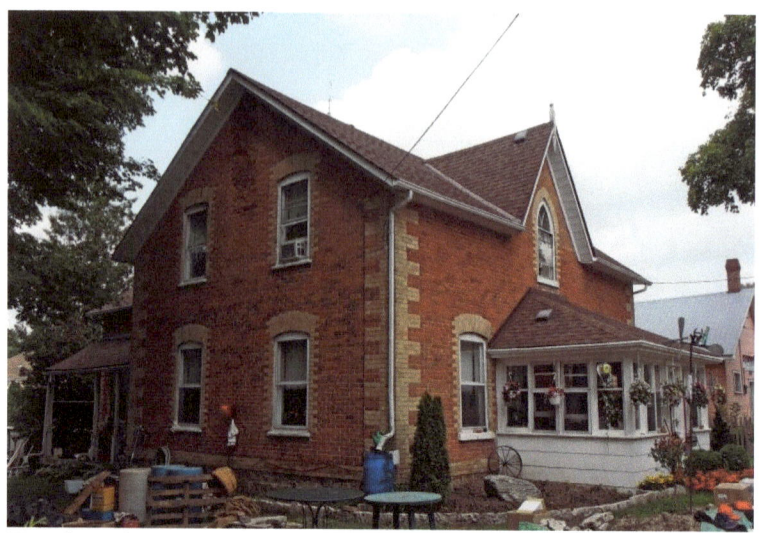

Frederick Street West – Gothic Revival, corner quoins, finial on gable

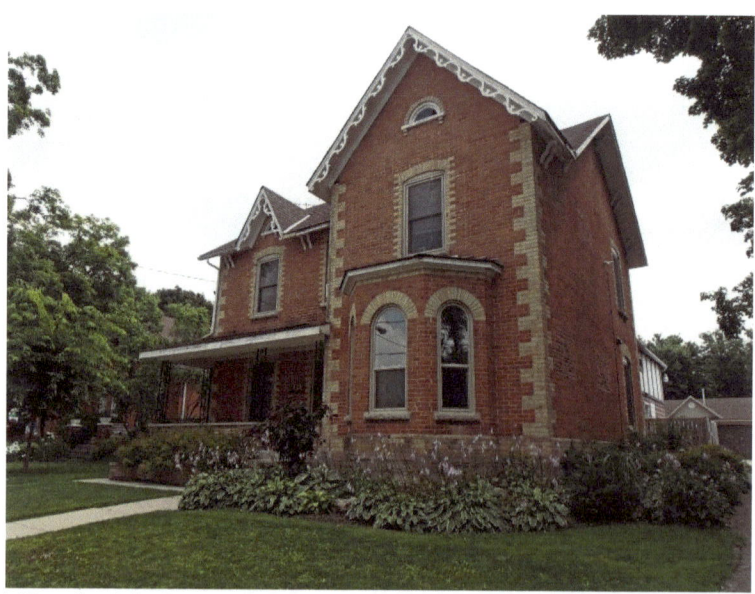

111 Frederick Street West – Gothic Revival, vergeboard trim on gables, corner quoins

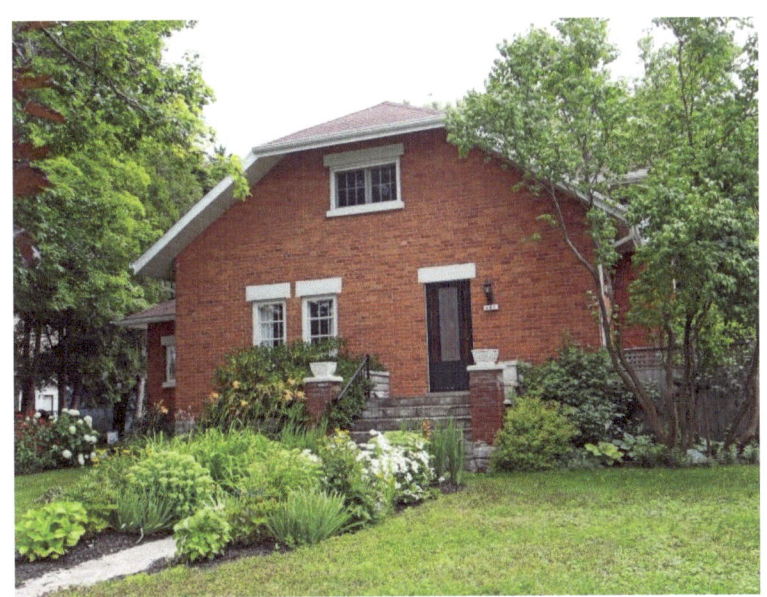

107 Frederick Street West

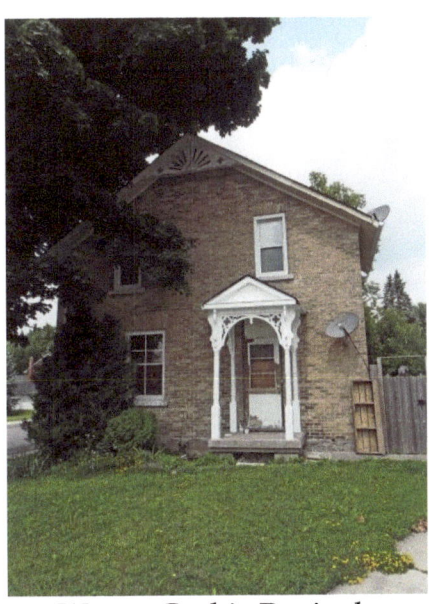

Frederick Street West – Gothic Revival, vergeboard trim

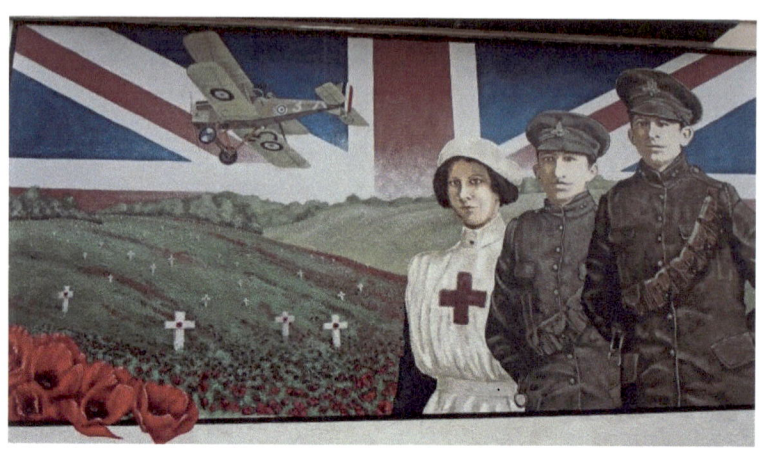

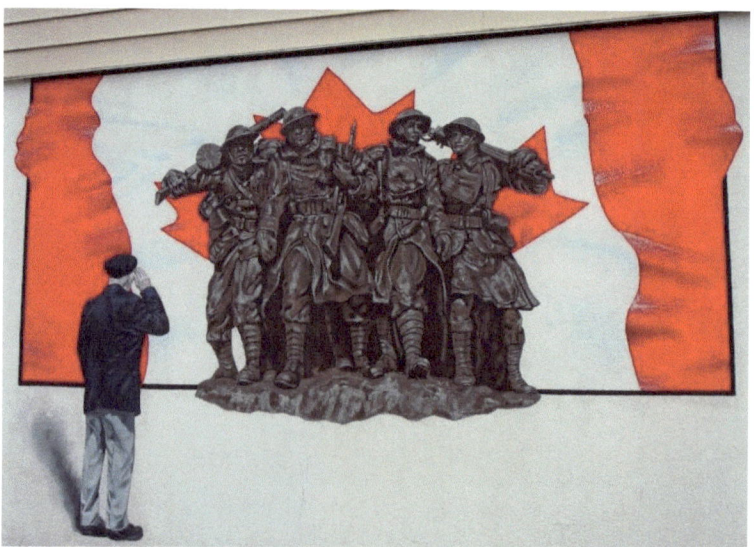

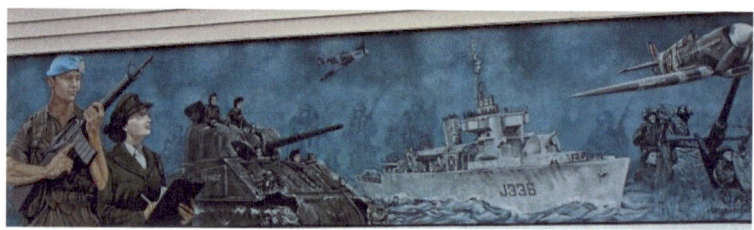

Veteran's Mural

The Veteran's Mural has three panels painted on the side wall of Sussman's at the corner of Frederick Street and Smith Street facing the United Church of Arthur. This mural is dedicated to the veterans of Arthur, male and female, who valiantly represented their village and country in the First and Second World Wars, and all conflicts since.

Arthur is recognized by the Ontario Provincial Legislature as being the Most Patriotic Village in Canada as one out of every seven Arthur residents fought in the Second World War. The first panel represents the First World War and contains two soldiers, a nurse, a WWI-era military biplane, and a military cemetery with poppies growing all set against a Union Jack. The middle panel was designed to represent the Second World War and is the recreation of local veteran John Walsh saluting the National War Memorial in Ottawa set against a Canadian flag. The third panel represents both WWII and all conflicts since 1945 in which Canadian soldiers have participated including Cyprus, the former Yugoslavia, Afghanistan, and Korea. This panel features a WWII-era mine sweeping ship, a female military officer, a UN peacekeeper a tank, an anti-aircraft gun and a Spitfire war plane.

This mural was painted by artist Cliff Smith.

These eye-catching memorials were designed to remind residents and visitors alike that the past should not be forgotten; especially not the absolute sacrifice soldiers make for freedom.

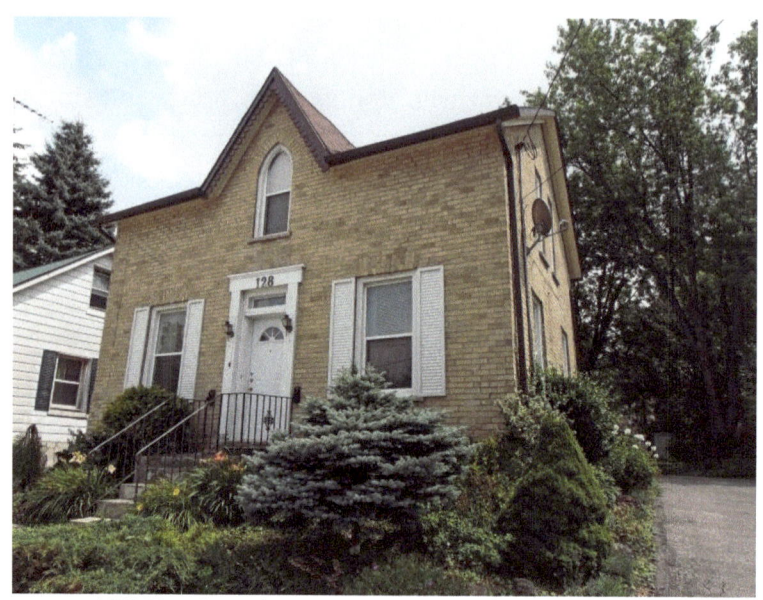

128 Frederick Street West – Gothic Revival

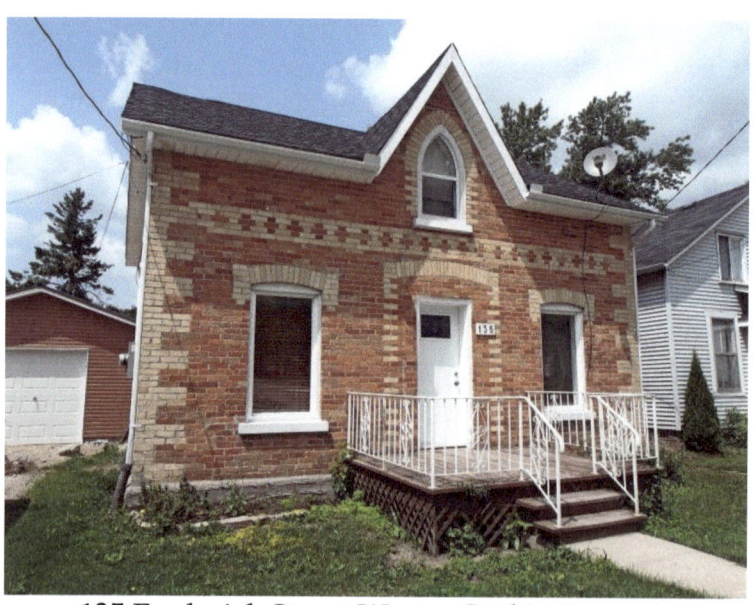

135 Frederick Street West – Gothic Revival,
dichromatic brickwork, corner quoins

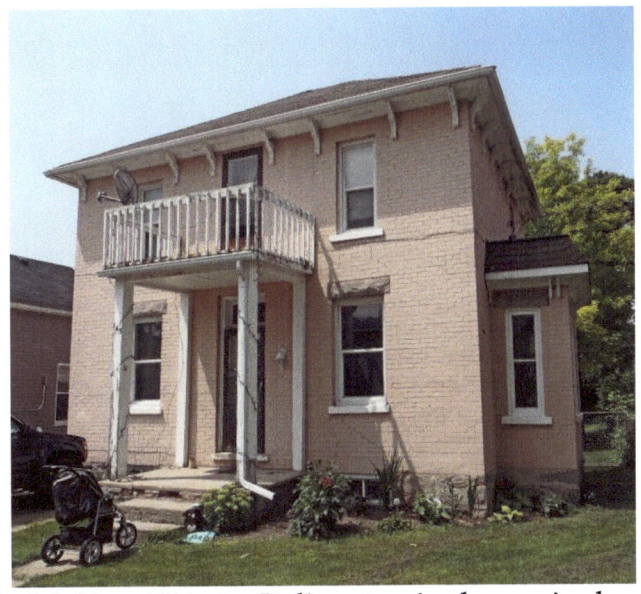

Frederick Street West – Italianate, single cornice brackets
Balcony on second floor

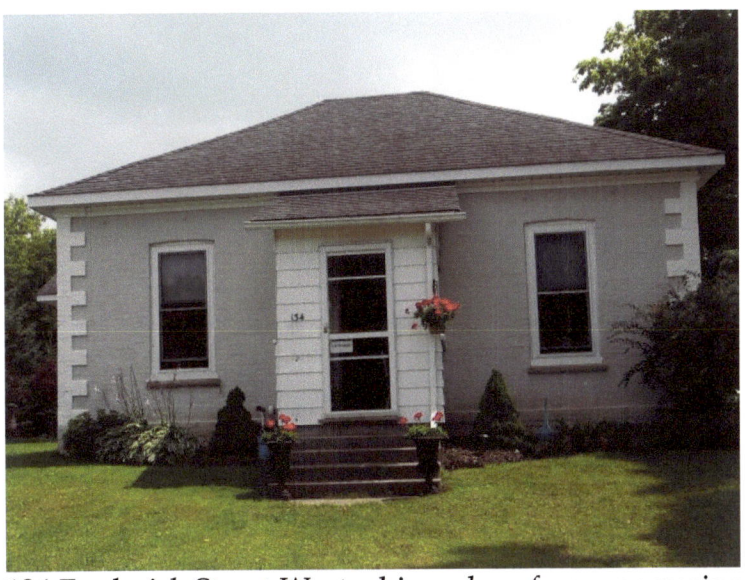

134 Frederick Street West – hipped roof, corner quoins

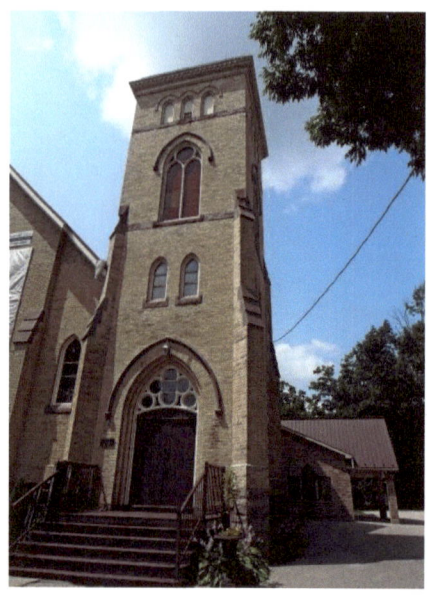

149 Frederick Street East - St. Andrew's Presbyterian Church

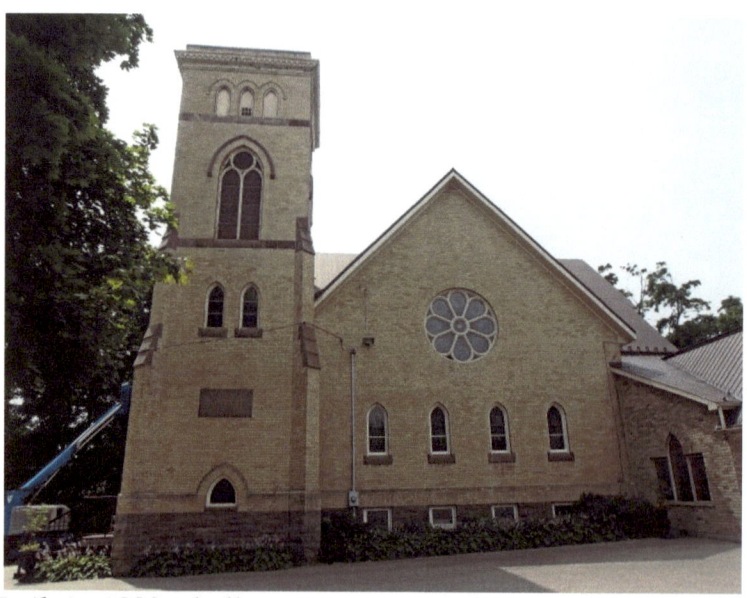

Built in 1899 – bell tower, rose window, lancet windows

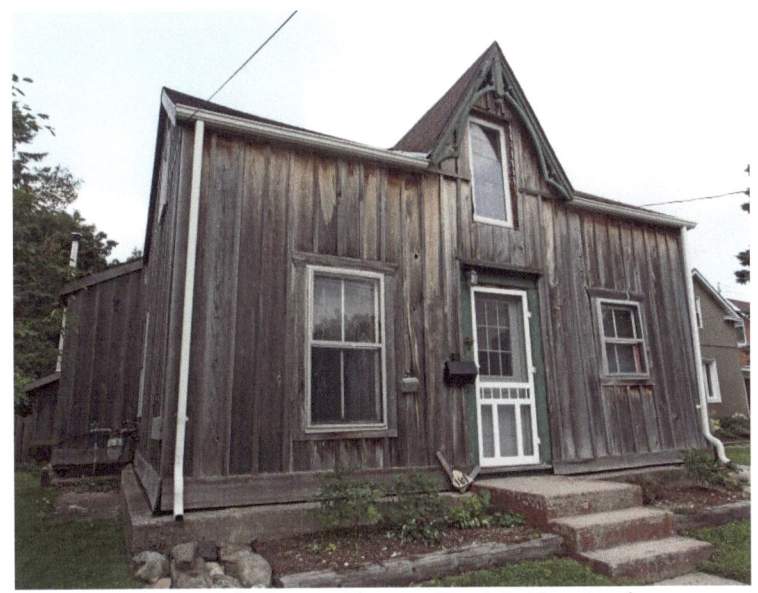

Frederick Street East – Gothic Revival,
vergeboard trim on gable

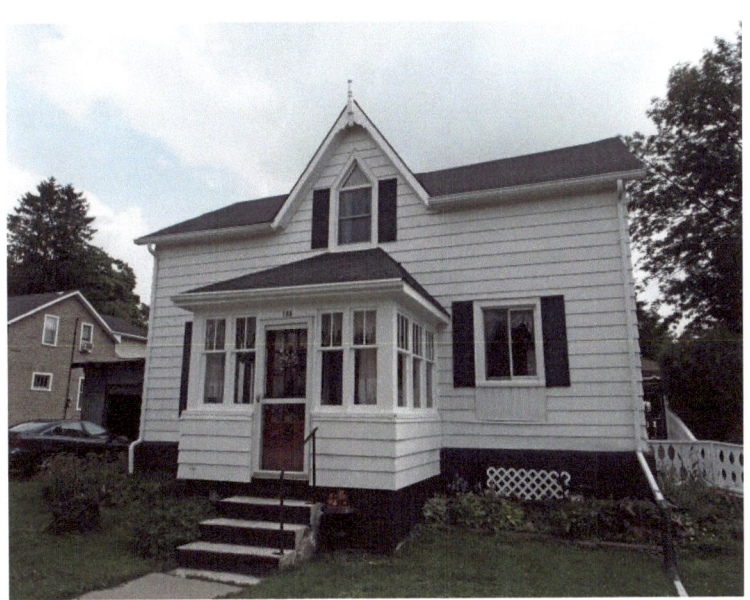

188 Frederick Street East – Gothic Revival, finial on gable

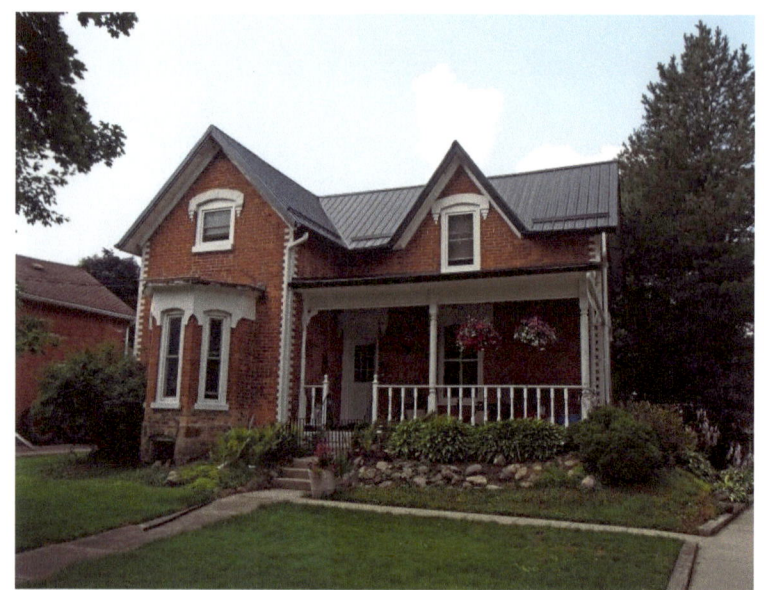

191 Frederick Street East – Gothic Revival, bay window
Corner quoins

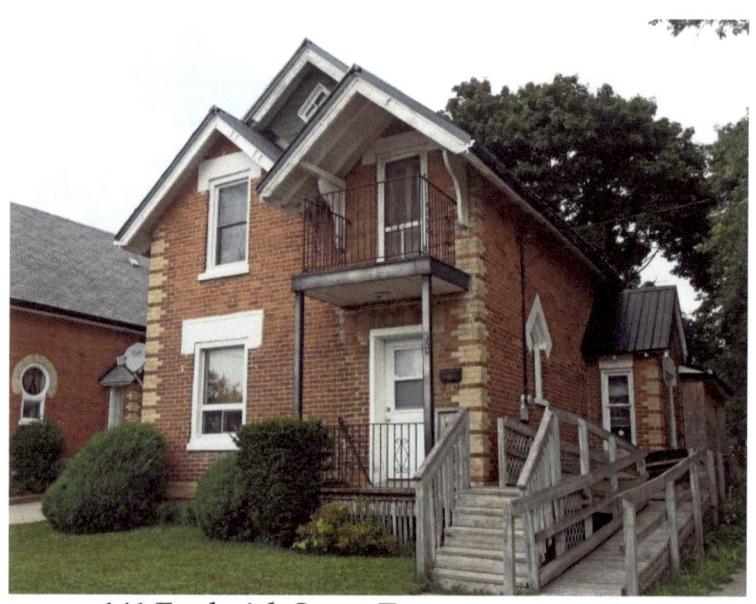

141 Frederick Street East – corner quoins

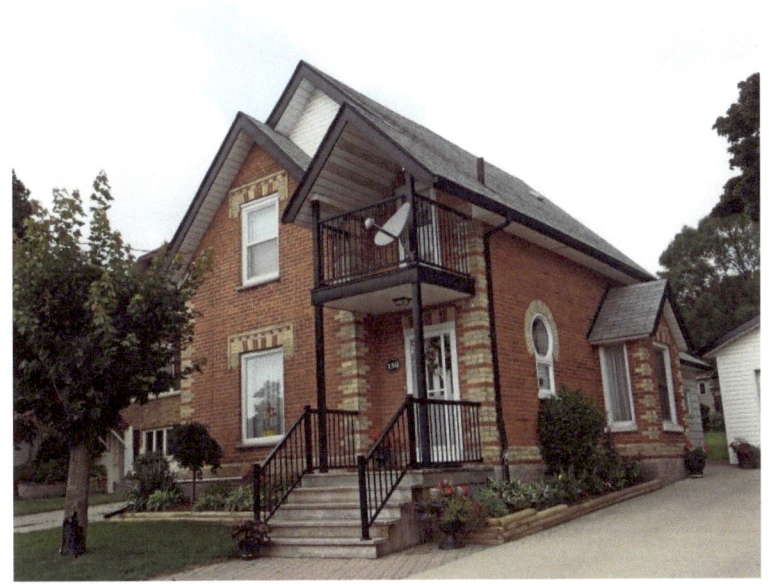

150 Frederick Street East – corner quoins

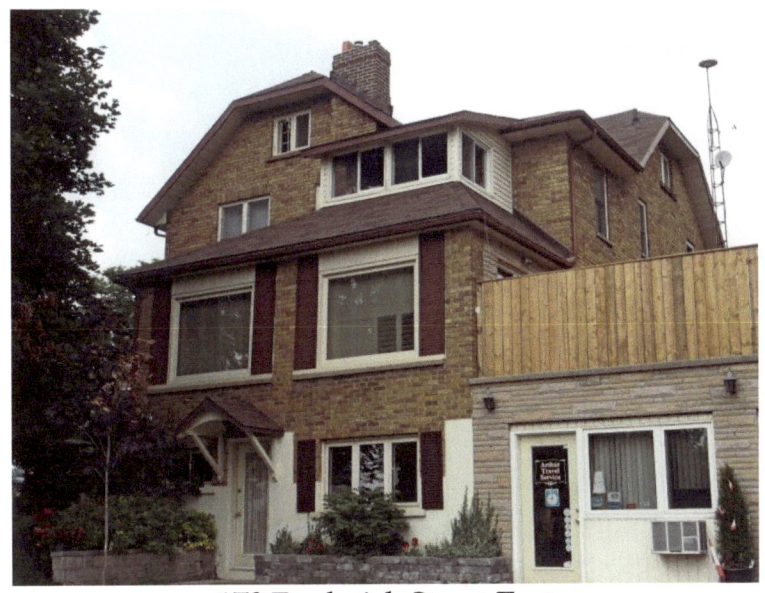

170 Frederick Street East

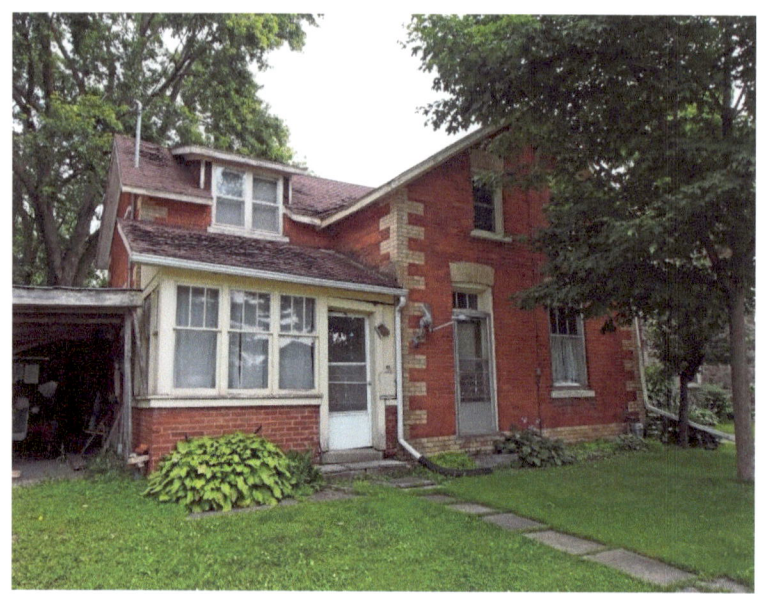

Isabella Street West - Gothic Revival, corner quoins

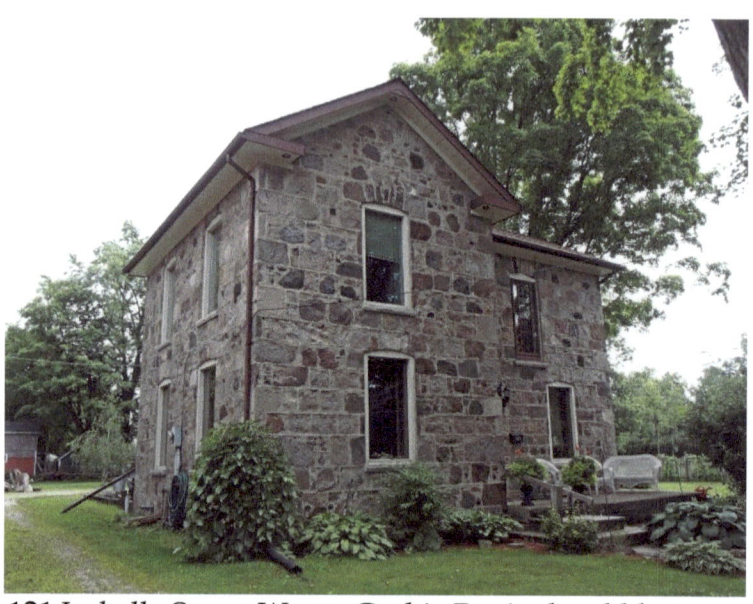

121 Isabella Street West - Gothic Revival, cobblestone, cornice return on gable

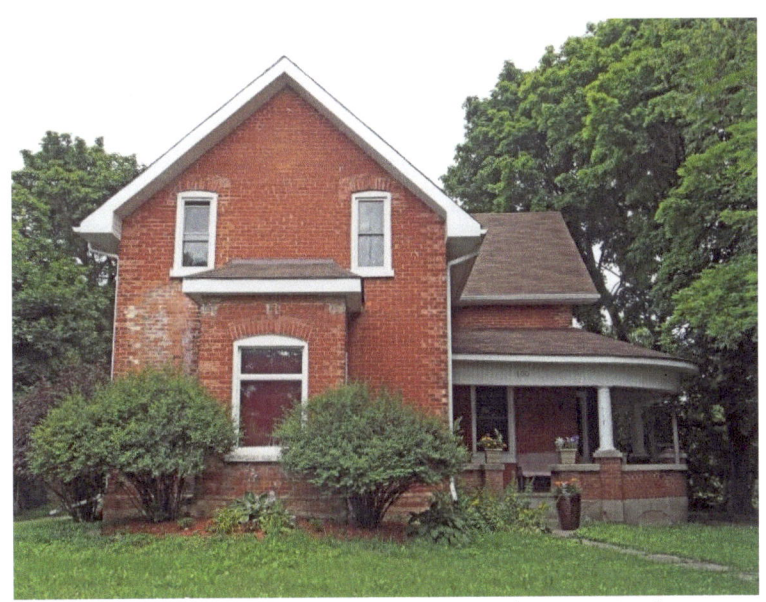

100 Isabella Street West - Gothic Revival

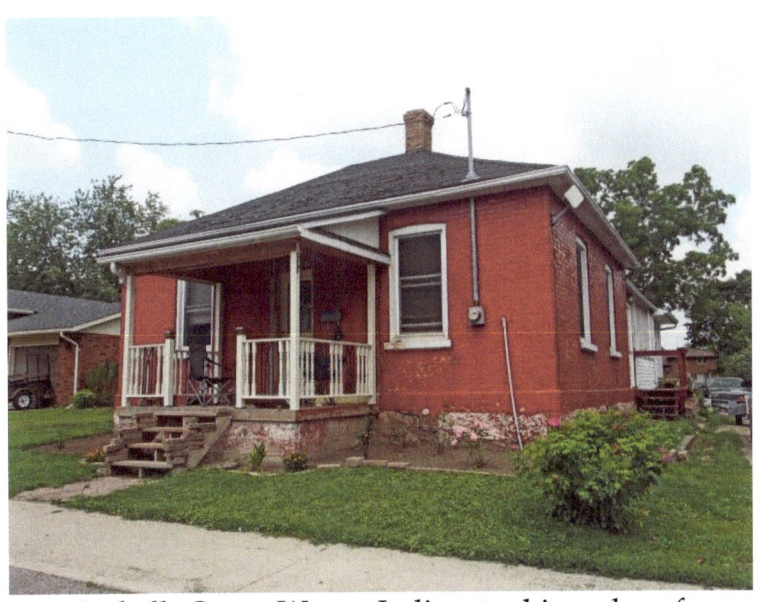

Isabella Street West – Italianate, hipped roof

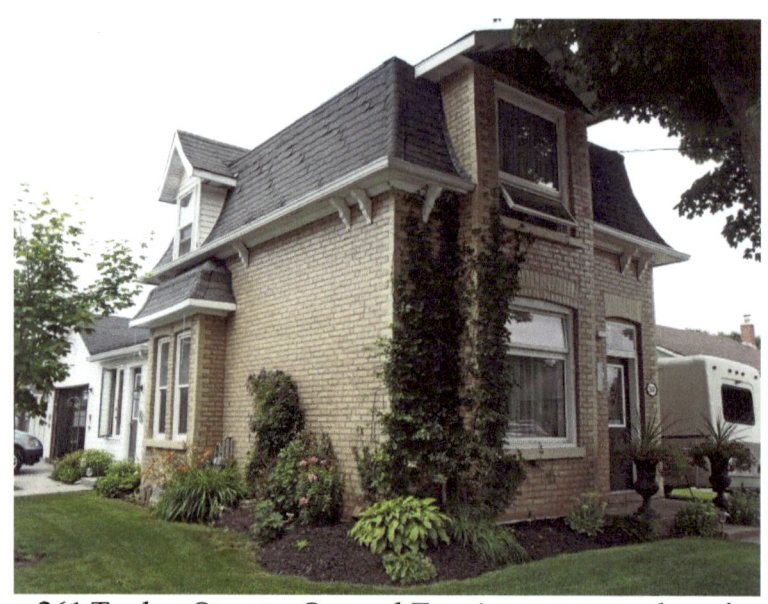

261 Tucker Street – Second Empire – mansard roof, Dormers, cornice brackets

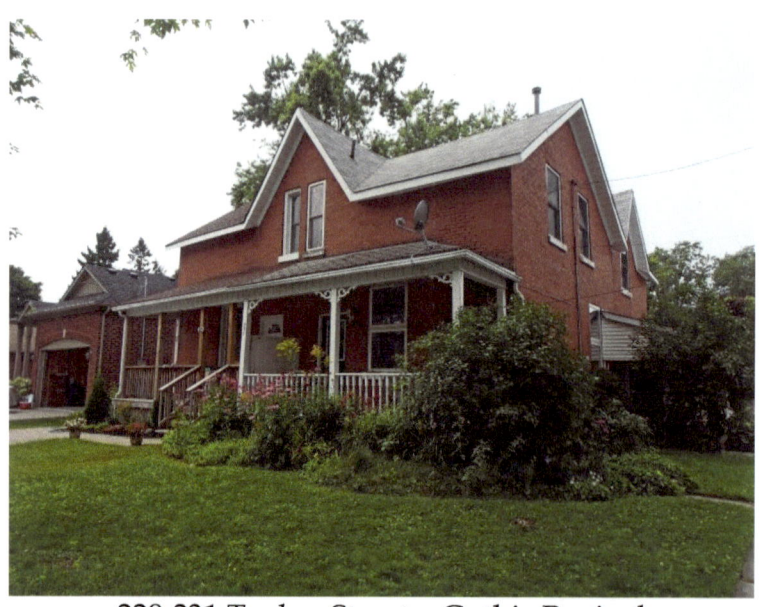

229-231 Tucker Street – Gothic Revival

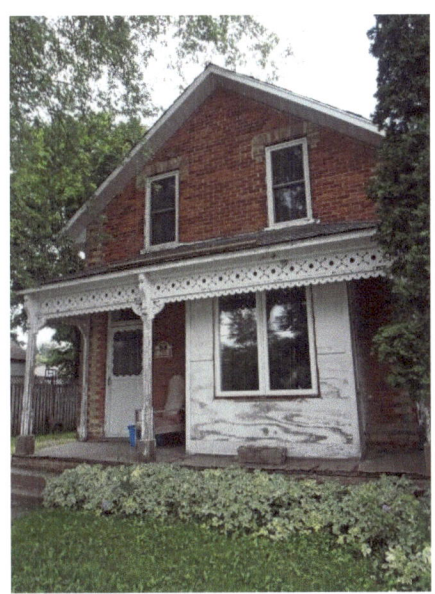

205 Tucker Street - Gothic

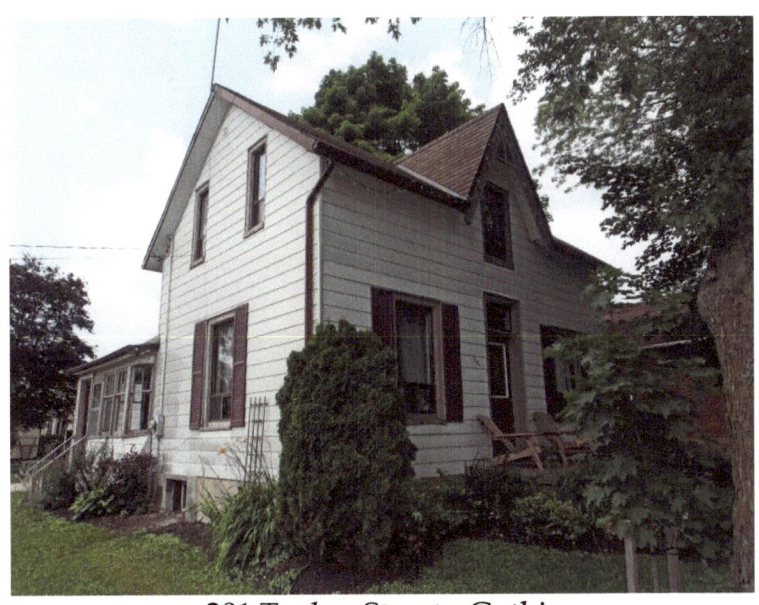

201 Tucker Street - Gothic

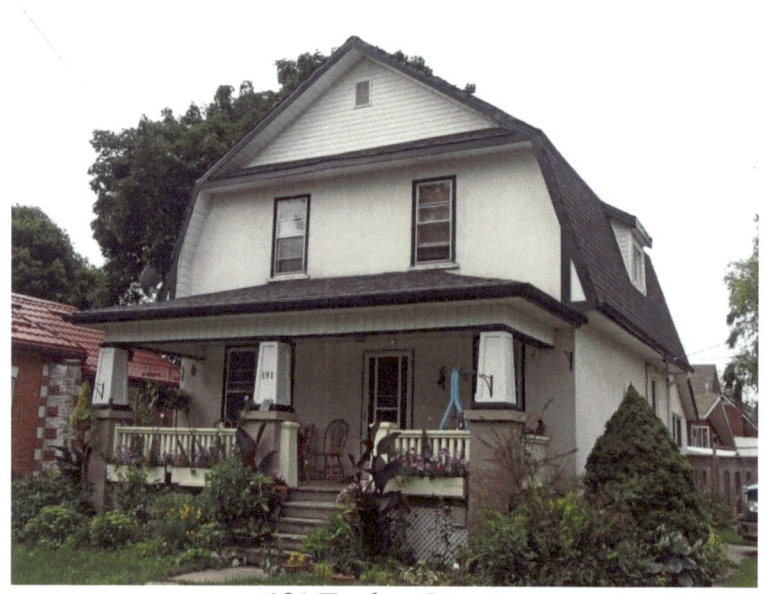

191 Tucker Street

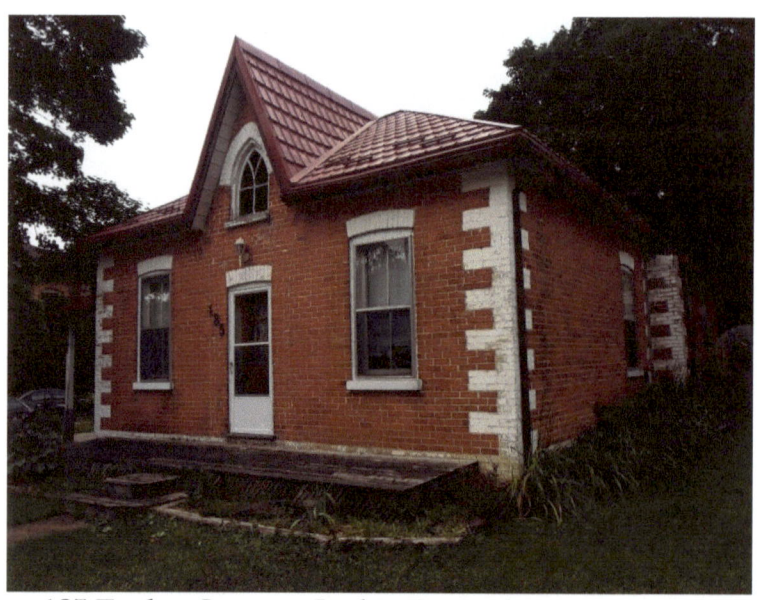

185 Tucker Street – Gothic Revival, corner quoins

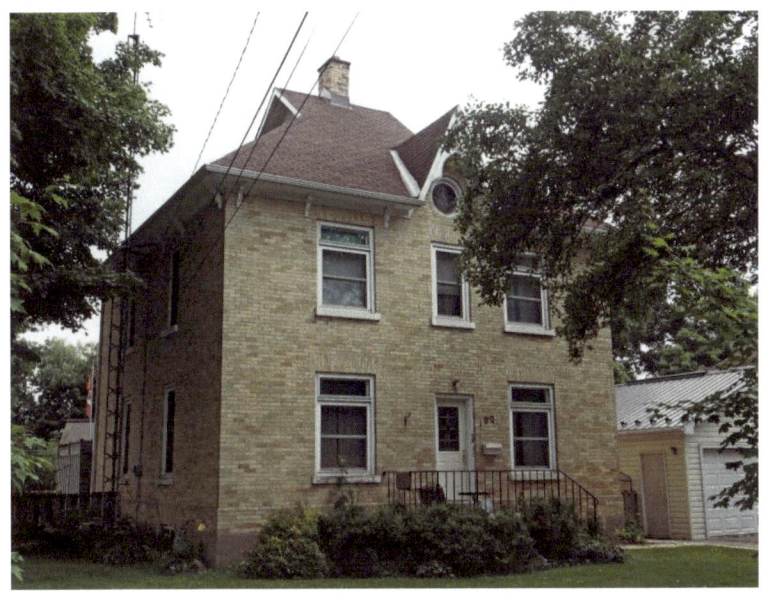

190 Tucker Street – local yellow brick, cornice brackets

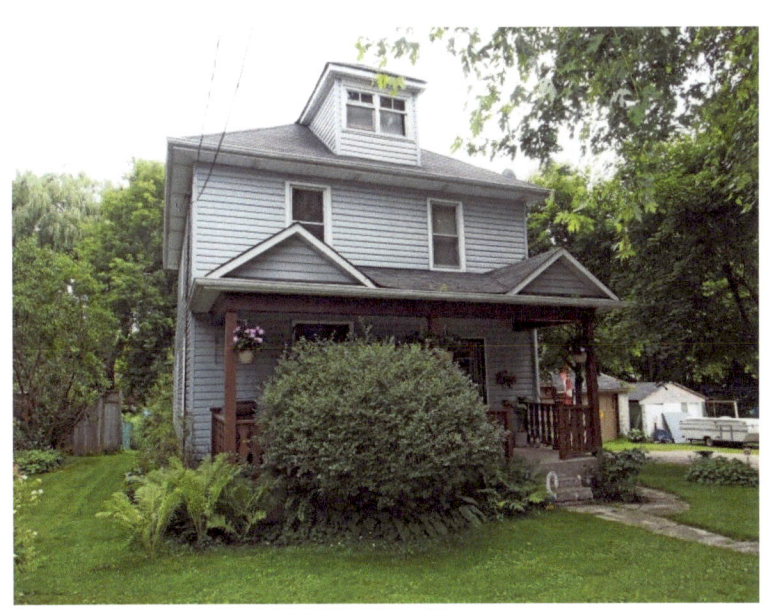

140 Tucker Street

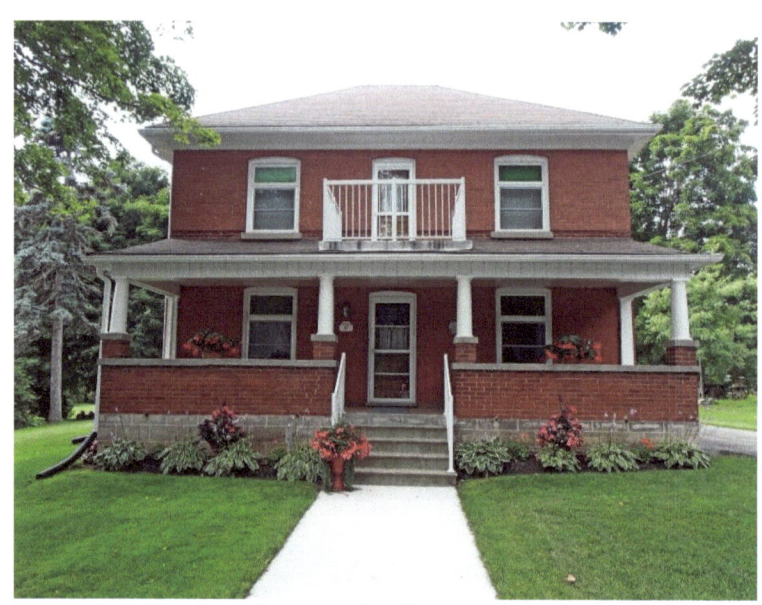

171 Tucker Street – Italianate, hipped roof,
balcony on second floor

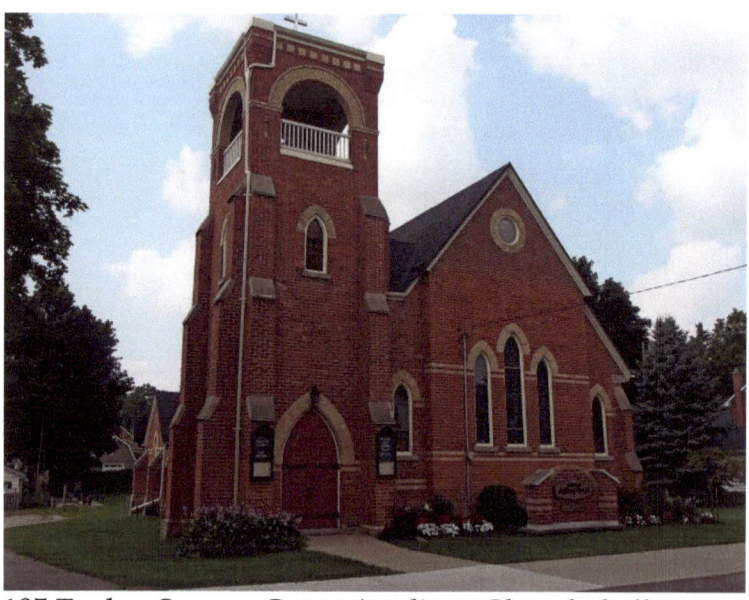

105 Tucker Street - Grace Anglican Church, bell tower,
buttresses, lancet windows

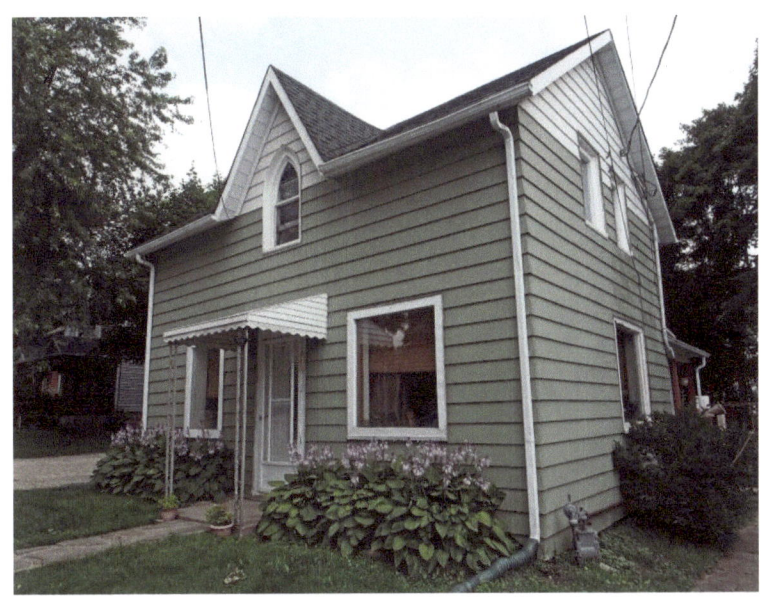

130 Tucker Street – Gothic Revival

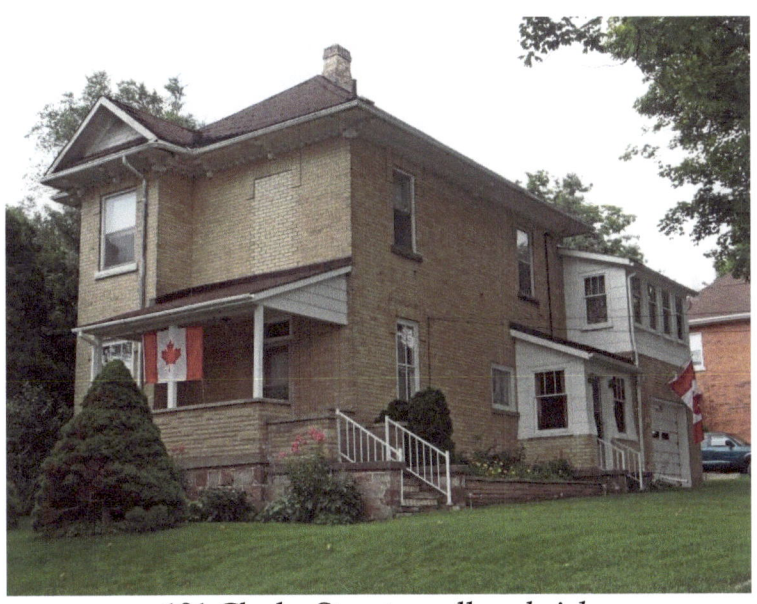

101 Clarke Street – yellow brick

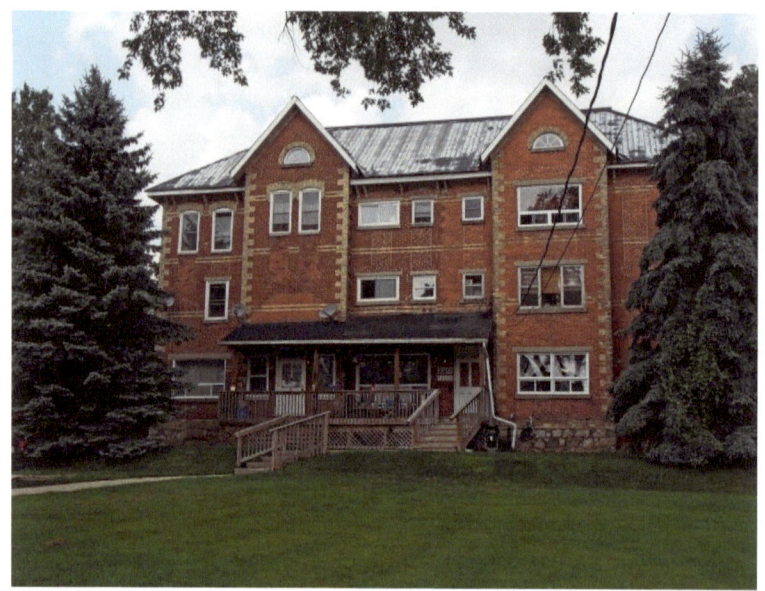

220 Smith Street – corner quoins, 3½ storey tower-like bays

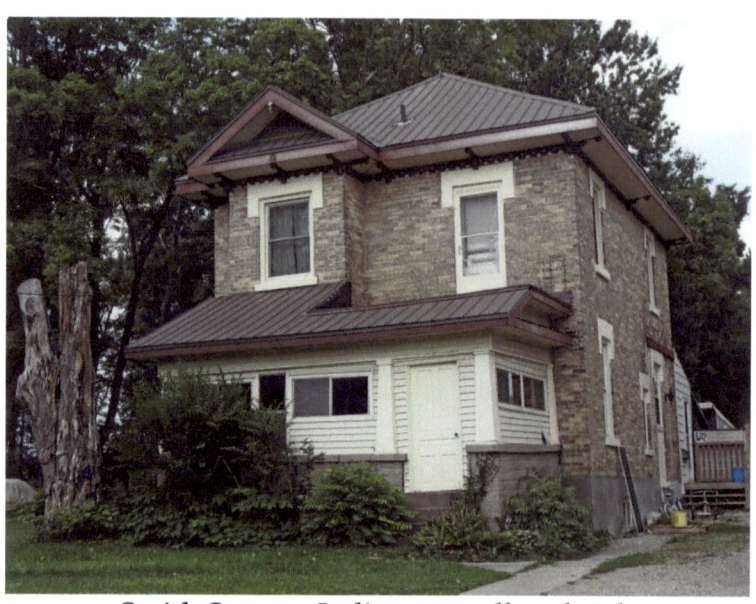

Smith Street – Italianate, yellow brick

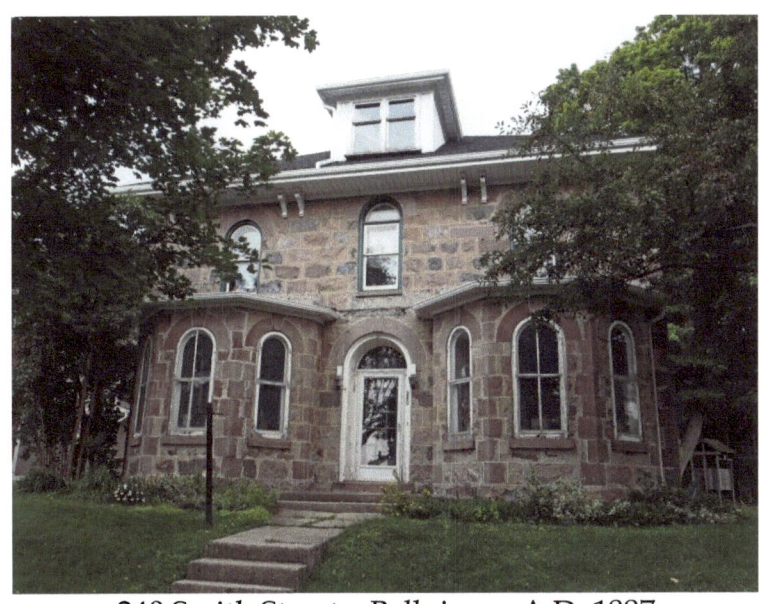

240 Smith Street – Bellview – A.D. 1887
Cobblestone architecture, bay windows, dormer on roof,
paired cornice brackets

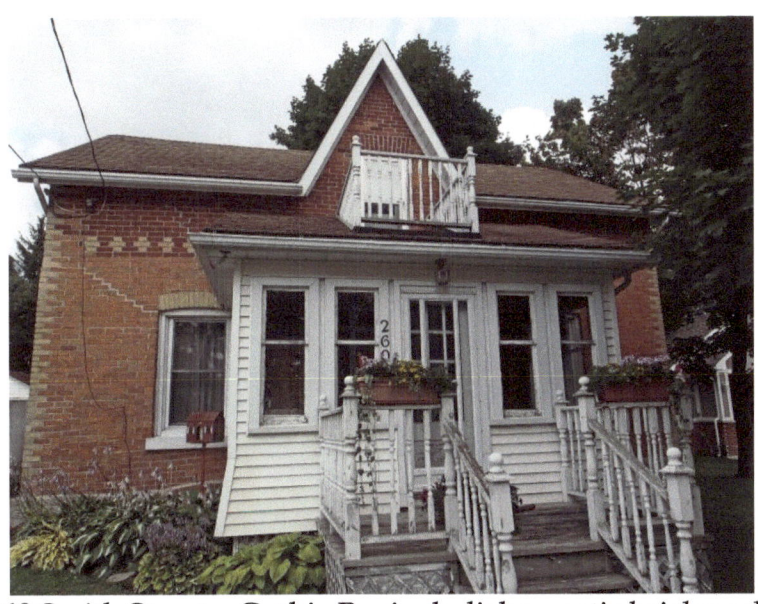

260 Smith Street – Gothic Revival, dichromatic brickwork,
corner quoins, balcony on second floor

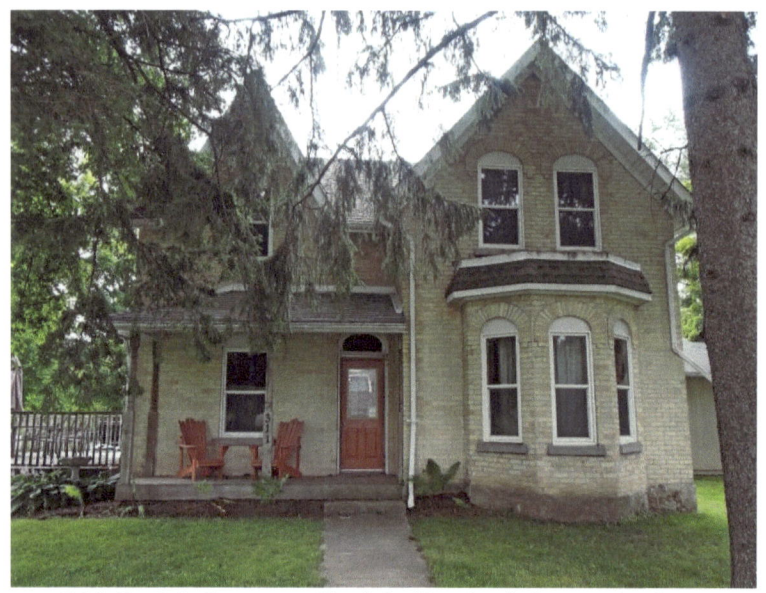

311 Smith Street – Gothic Revival, bay window

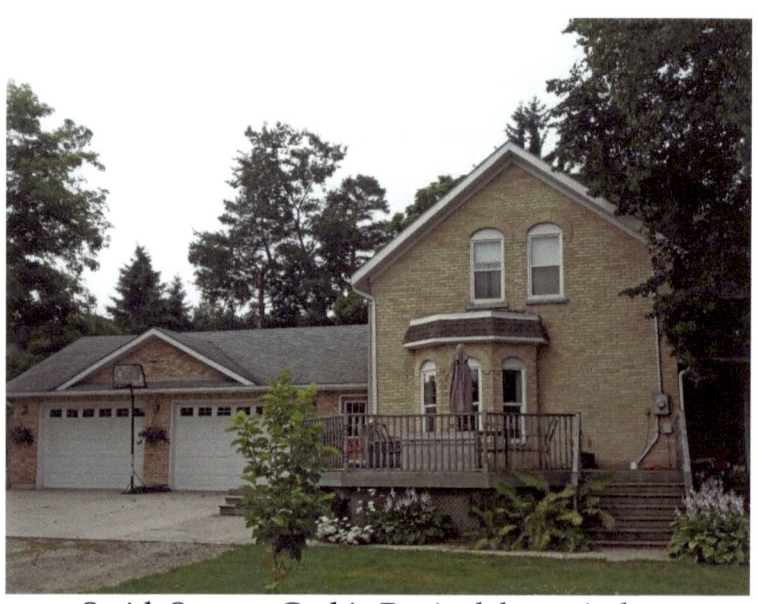

Smith Street – Gothic Revival, bay window

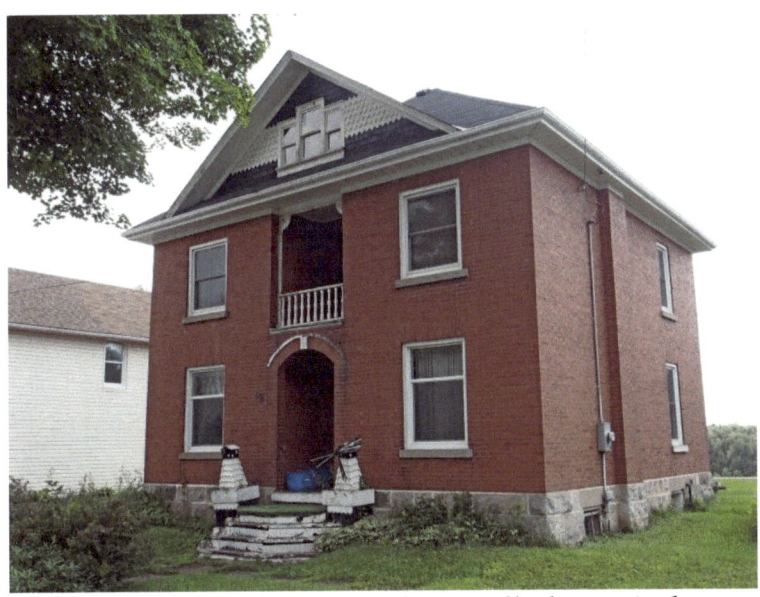

291 Smith Street – Edwardian, Palladian window

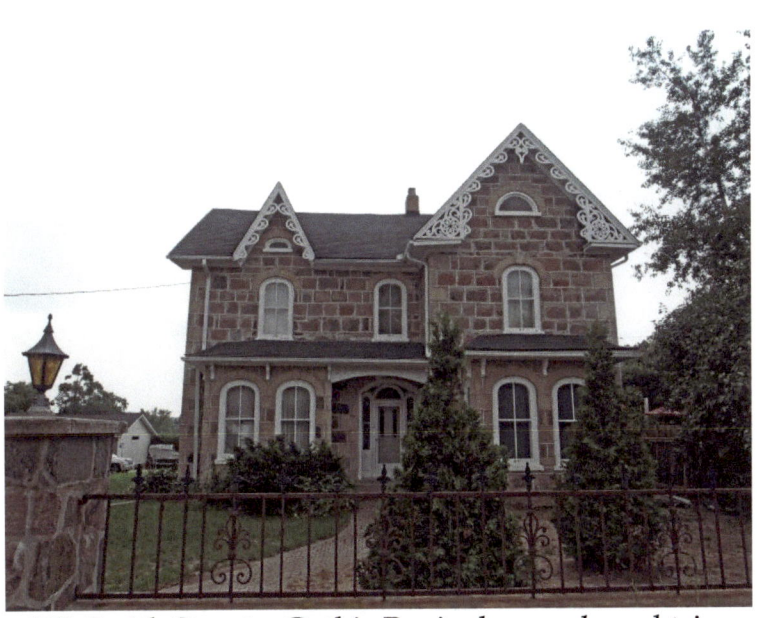

271 Smith Street – Gothic Revival, vergeboard trim
and finial on gables, cobblestone architecture,
bay windows, cornice brackets

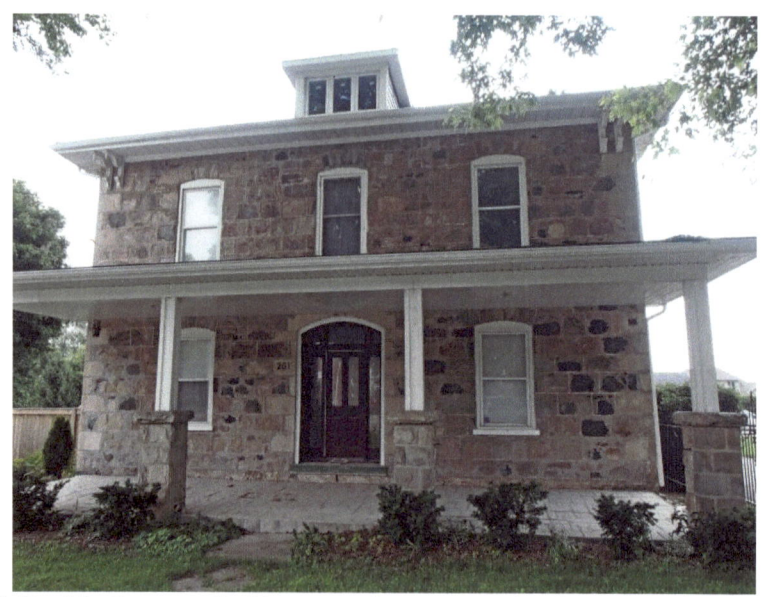

261 Smith Street – Italianate, dormer, paired cornice brackets, cobblestone architecture

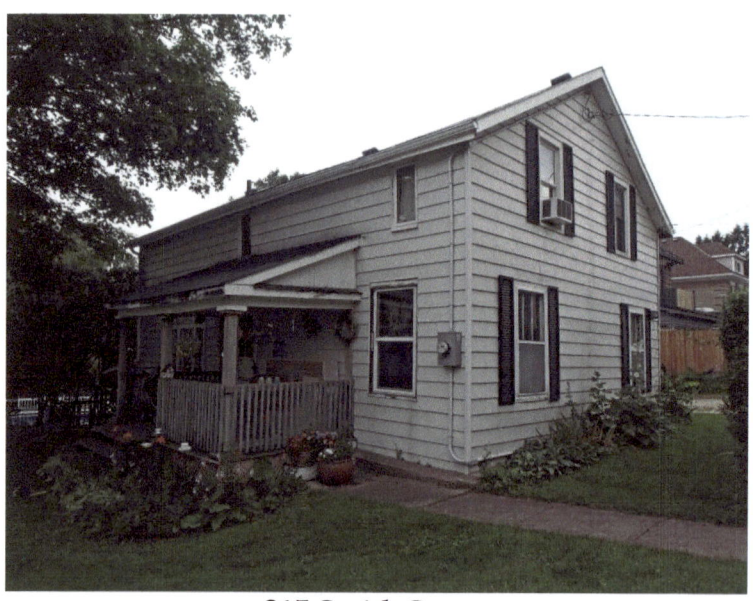

215 Smith Street

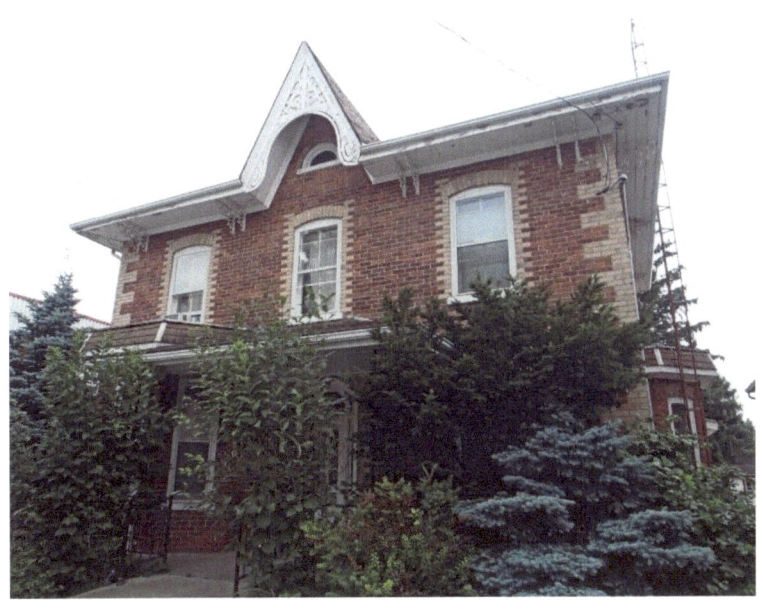

137 Smith Street – Gothic Revival, vergeboard trim,
dichromatic brickwork, corner quoins, cornice brackets

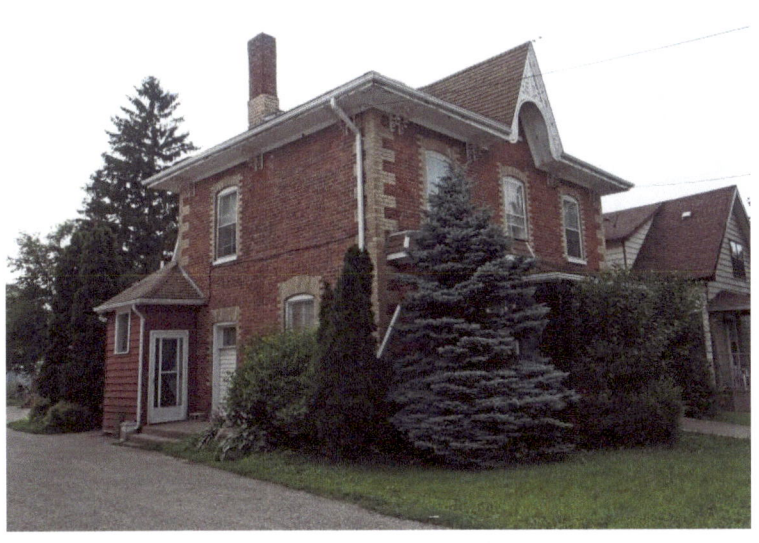

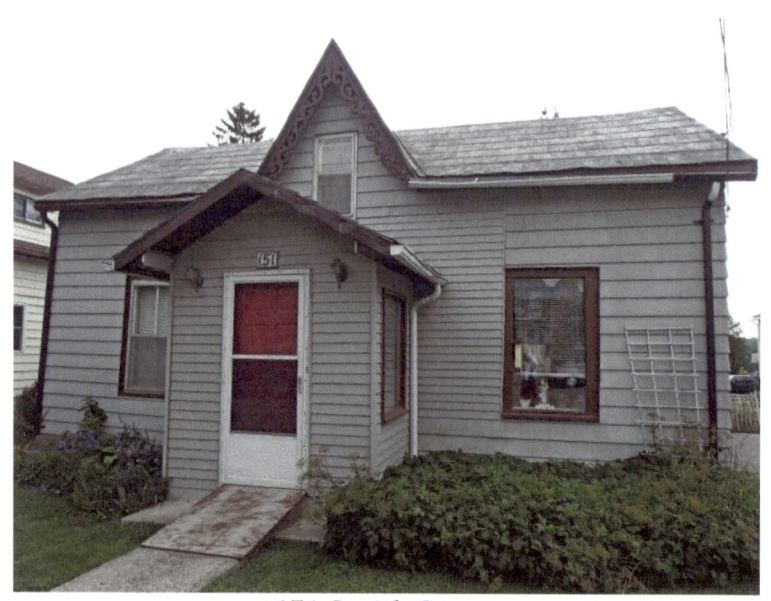

151 Smith Street

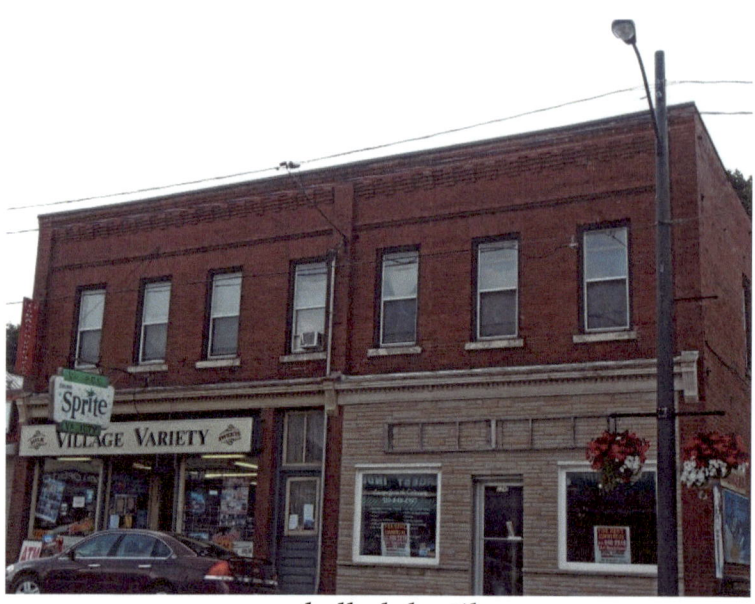

corbelled dentils

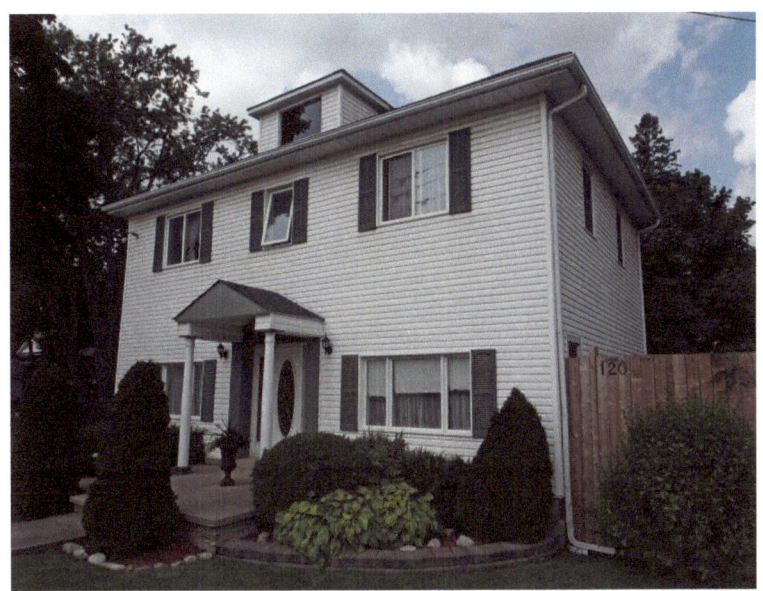

120 Smith Street – Italianate, dormer

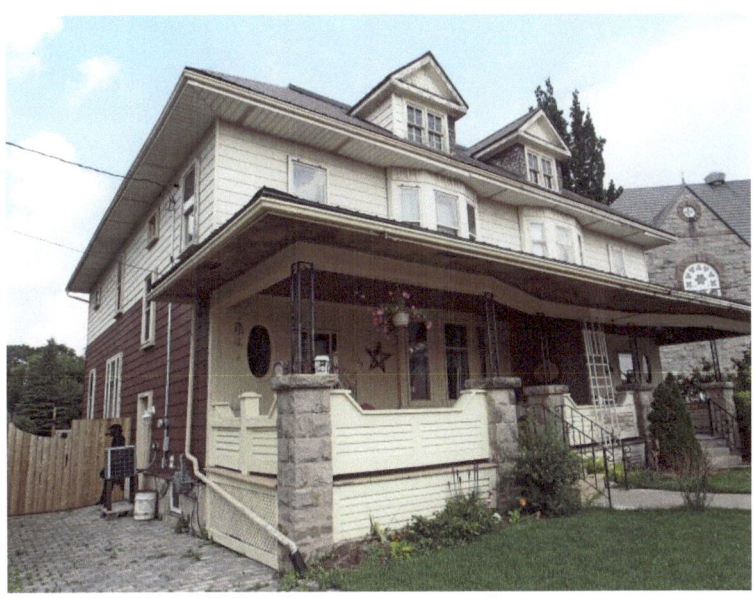

110 Smith Street – two dormers

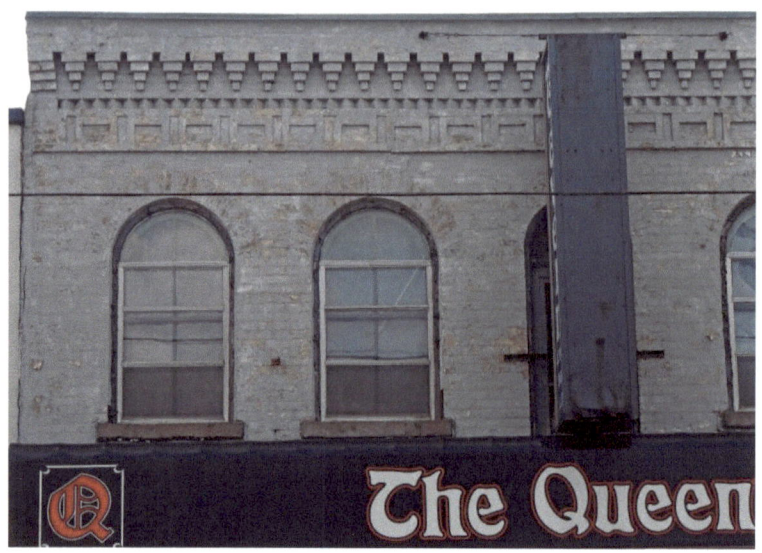

164 George Street - The Queens Tavern

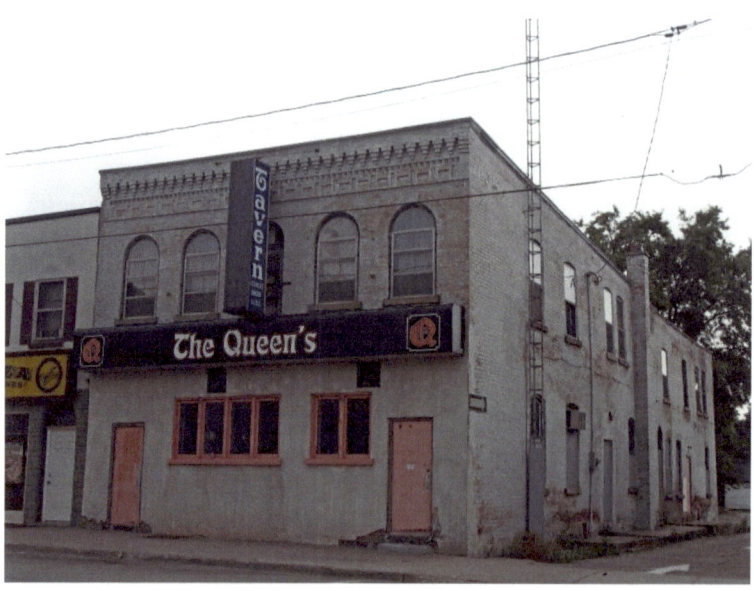

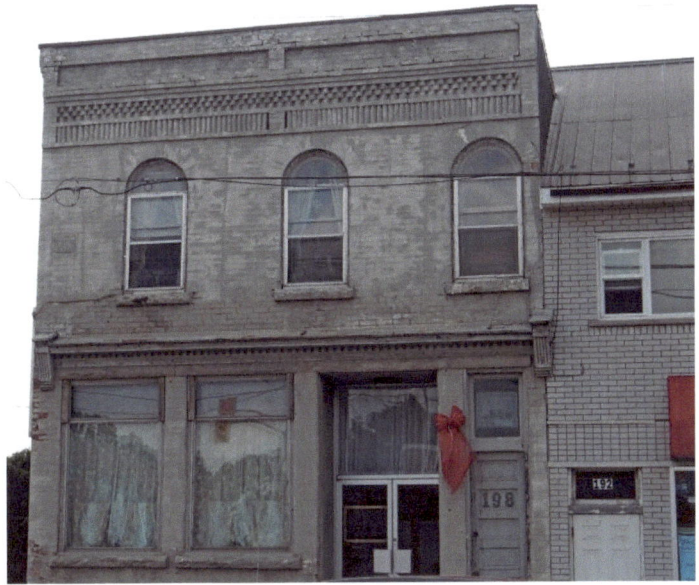

Dentil moulding

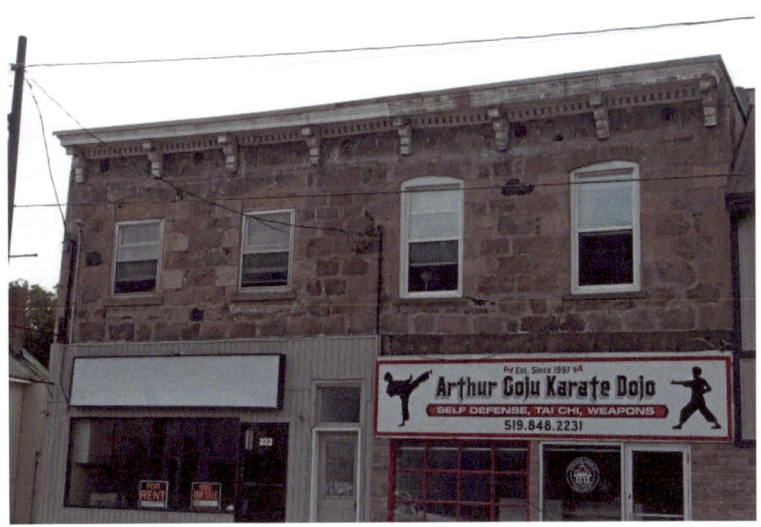

Cornice brackets, cobblestone architecture

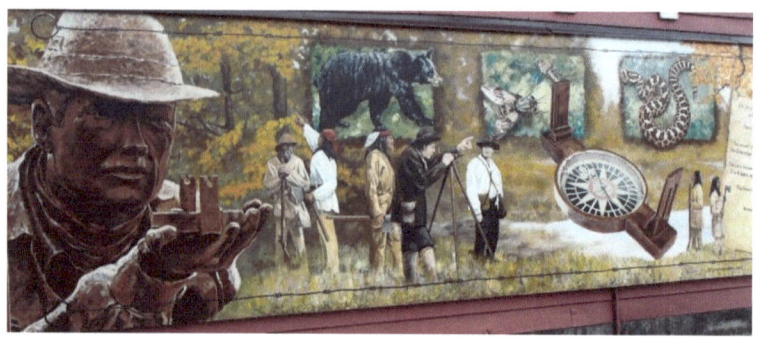

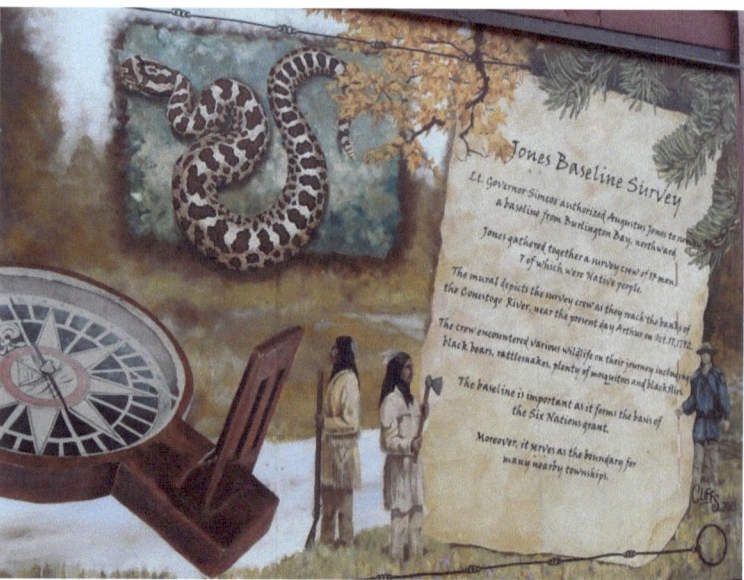

Jones Baseline Survey mural is mounted on the side of the 2nd Look store, on the corner of George and Charles Streets.

Lt. Governor Simcoe authorized Augustus Jones to survey a baseline from Burlington Bay northward. Jones gathered together a survey team of thirteen men, seven of whom were native people. The mural depicts the survey crew as they reach the banks of the Conestogo River near the present day Arthur on August 17, 1792. The crew encountered many impediments to their progress ranging from dense bush, swamps, uneven terrain, and wildlife including black bears, and rattlesnakes, with plenty of mosquitoes and blackflies. The baseline forms the basis of the Six Nations grant, and it serves as the boundary for many nearby townships.

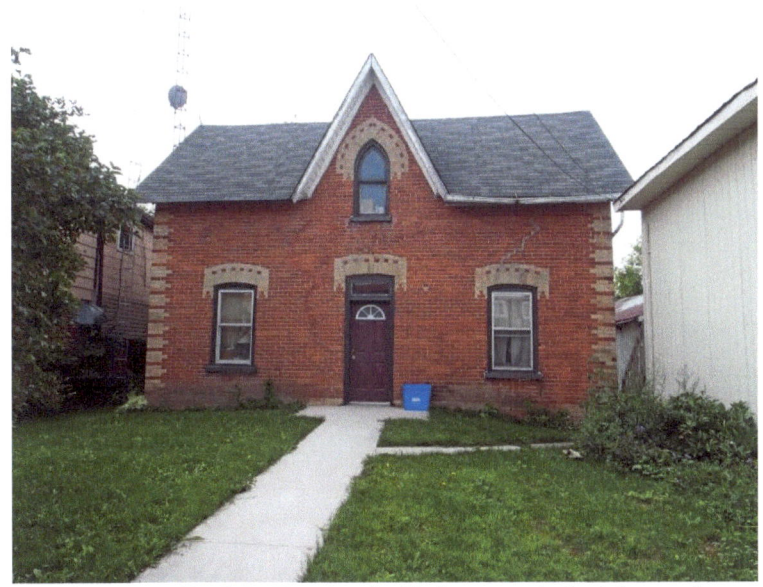

George Street – Gothic Revival, dichromatic brickwork, corner quoins

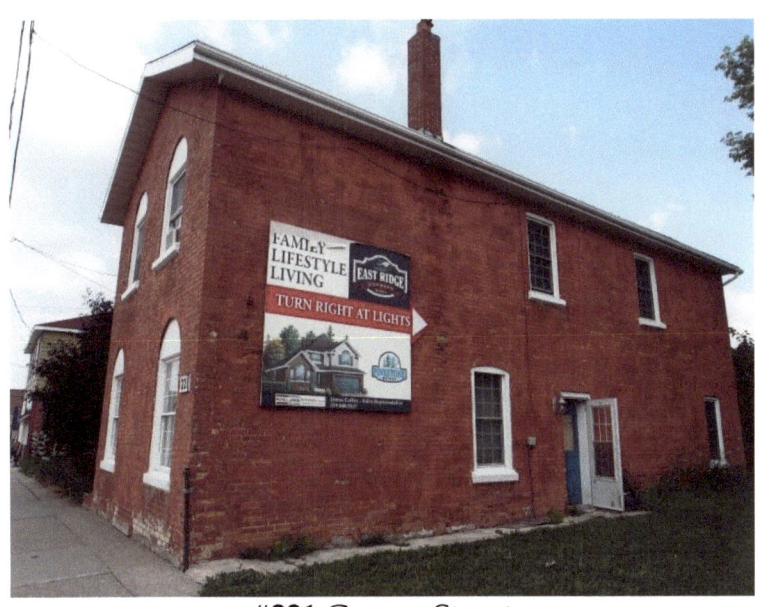

#221 George Street

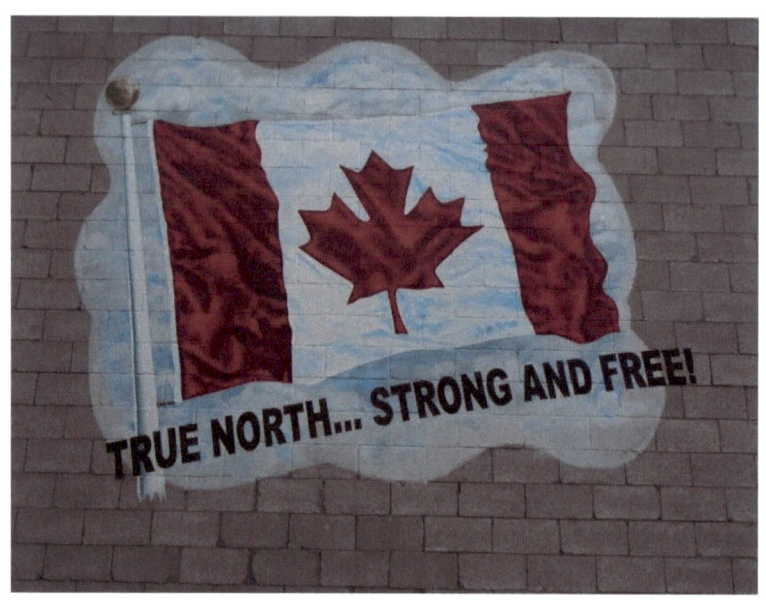

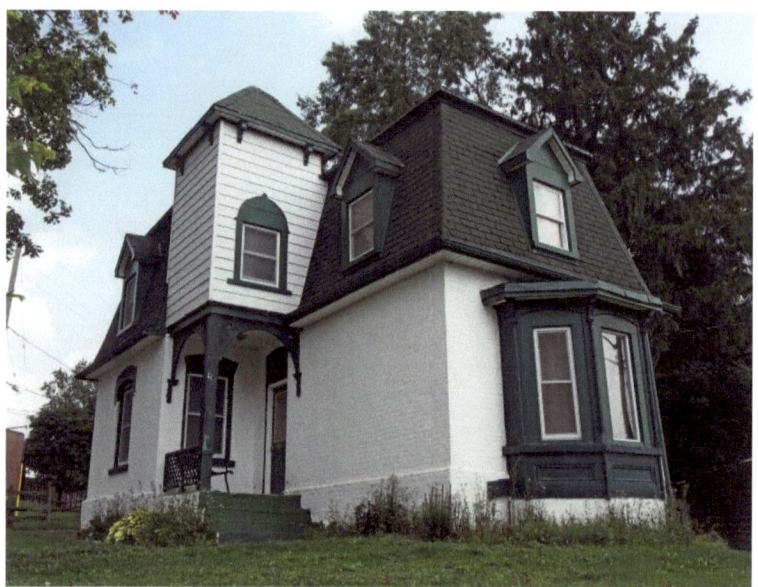

#301 – Second Empire – mansard roof with dormers, bay window, square turret above porch

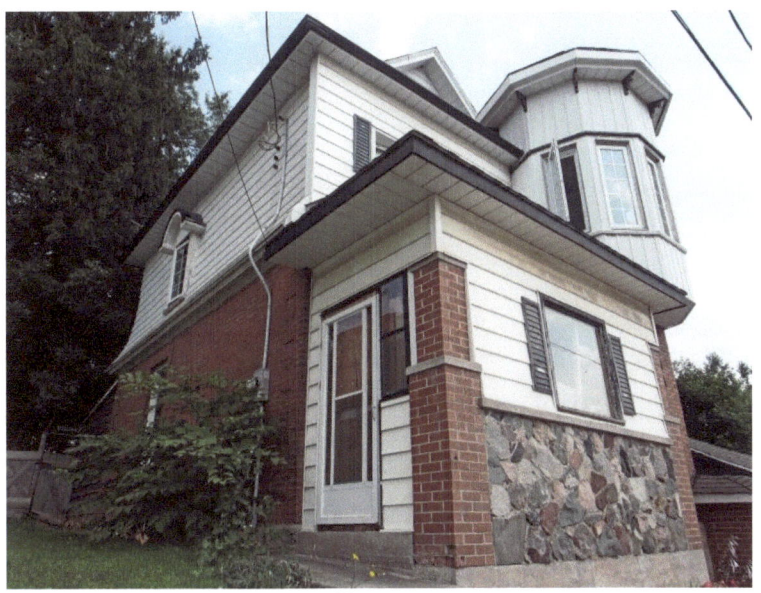

Turret

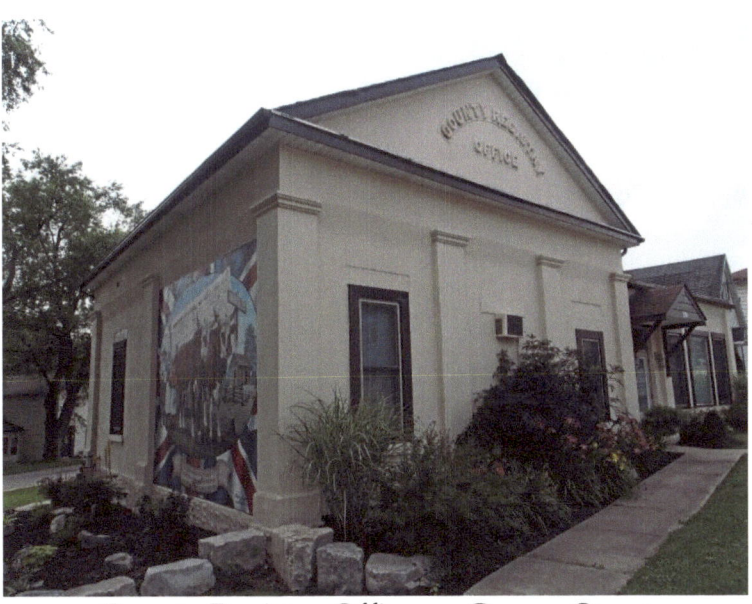

County Registry Office on George Street

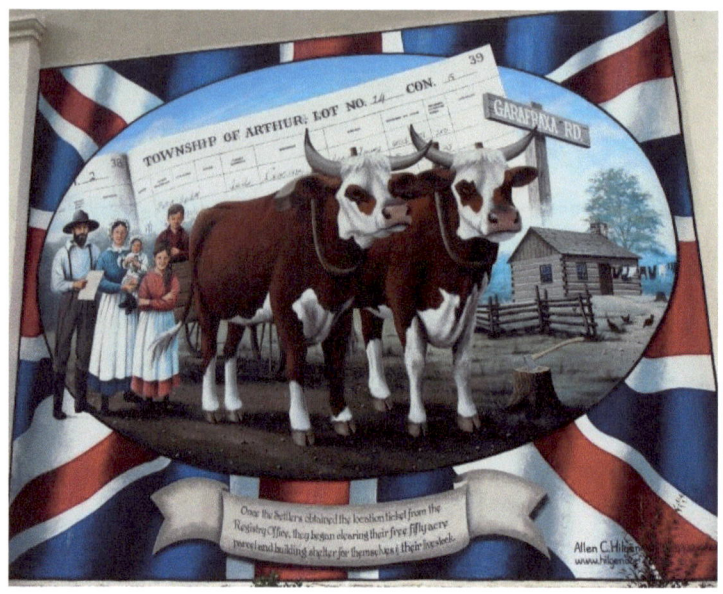

The Pioneer Mural in Arthur is painted on the South wall of the Hunter Tax Management Office at the southern entrance to the village. The location of this mural is symbolic as this office building is the former County Registry Office.

The mural depicts an early settler departing from the Registry Office with family and his yoke of oxen. The settler has in his hands his 'location papers' which entitles him to a free fifty-acre plot of land in Arthur Township. To reach his property he would have travelled north on the Garafraxa Road, what is now Highway 6.

This was the first of several murals commissioned by the Arthur Mural Committee and was designed and painted by artist Allen C.Hilgendorf.

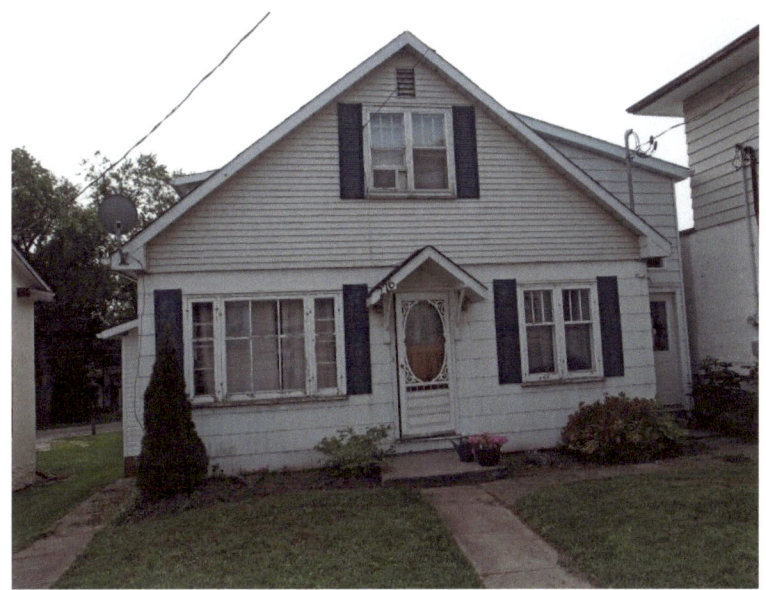

#276 George Street

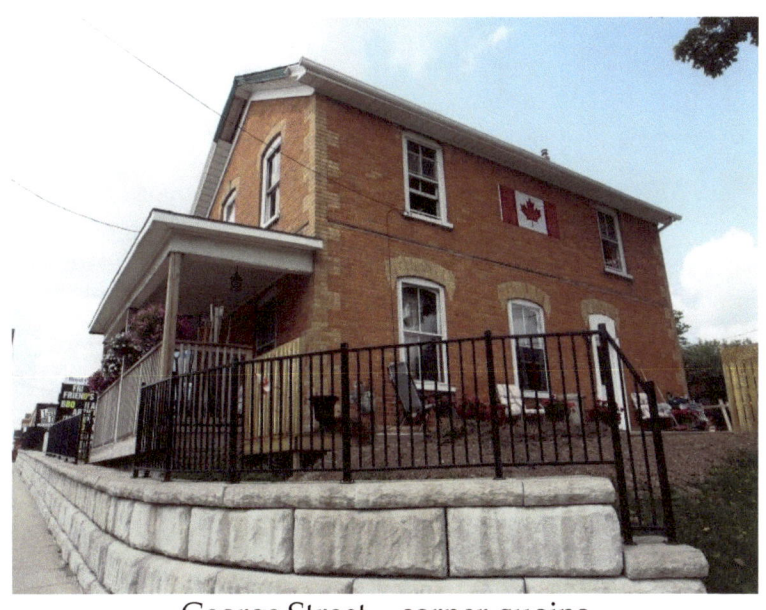

George Street – corner quoins

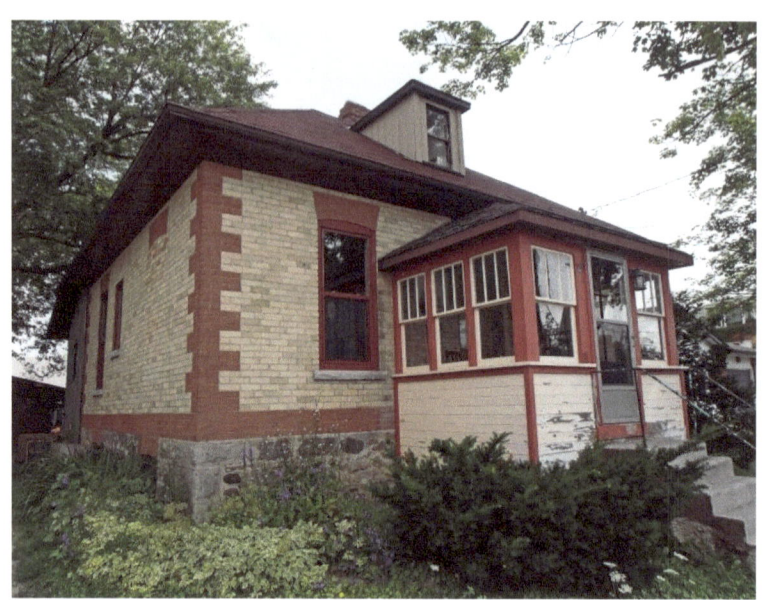

271 Isabella Street East

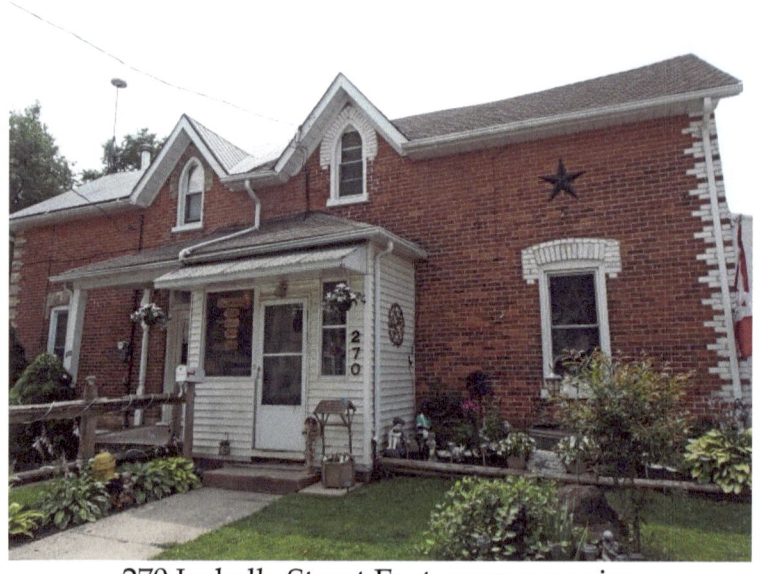

270 Isabella Street East, corner quoins

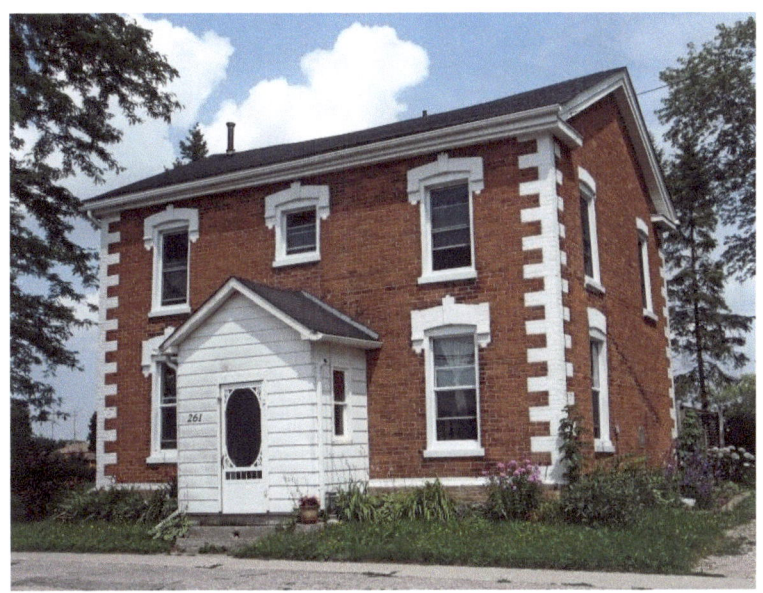

261 Isabella Street East – corner quoins
Window architraves with keystones

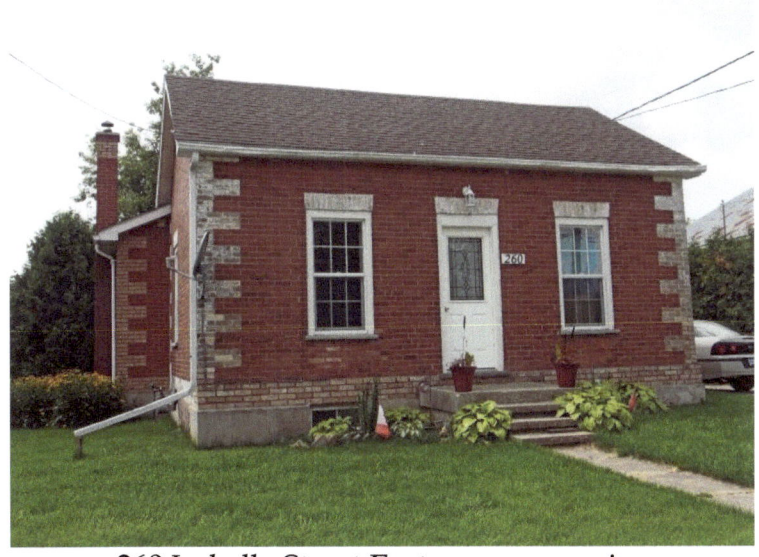

260 Isabella Street East – corner quoins

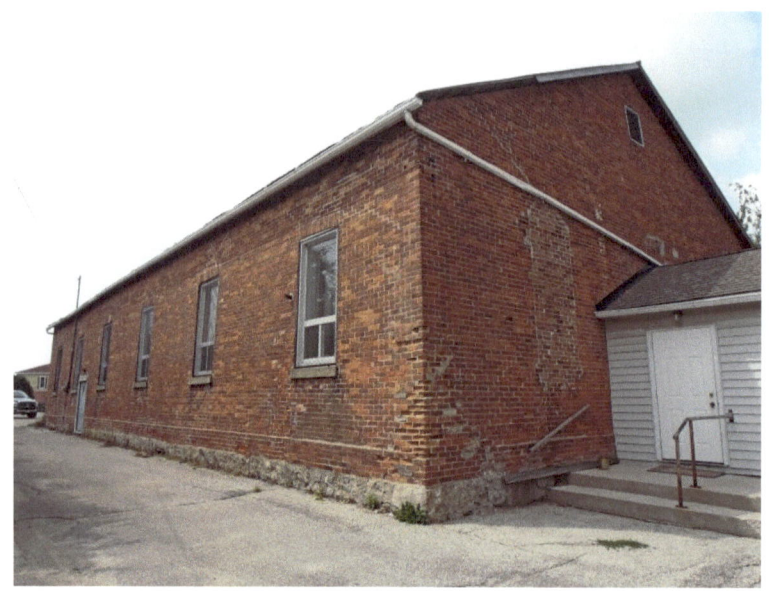

244 Isabella Street East, Senior Citizen Hall

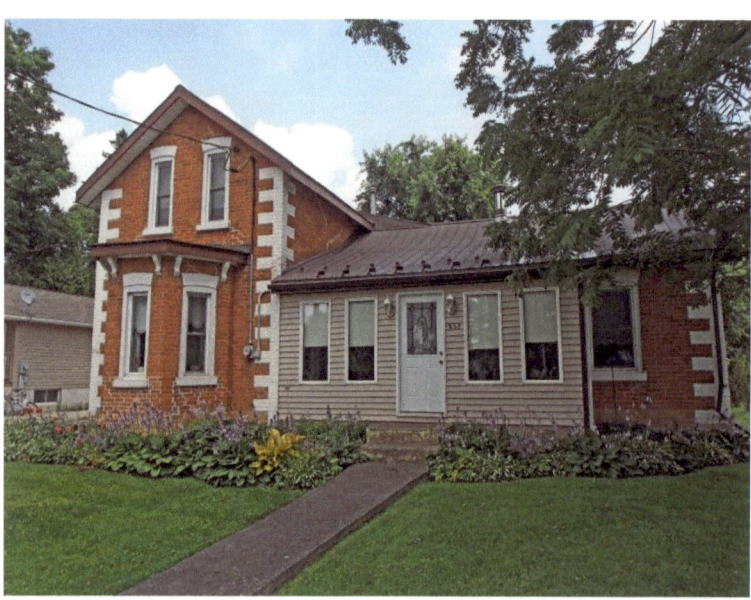

221 Isabella Street East – Gothic Revival, corner quoins, bay window, cornice brackets

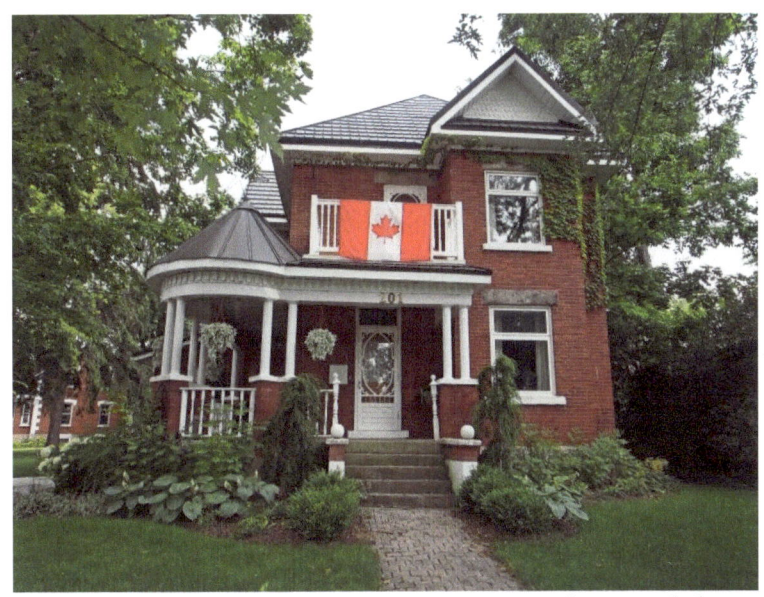

201 Isabella Street East – wraparound verandah

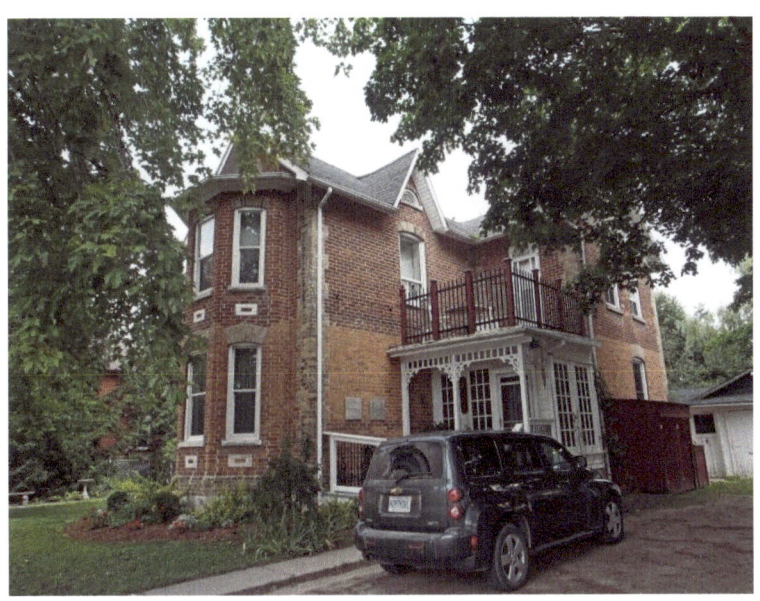

Isabella Street East – corner quoins

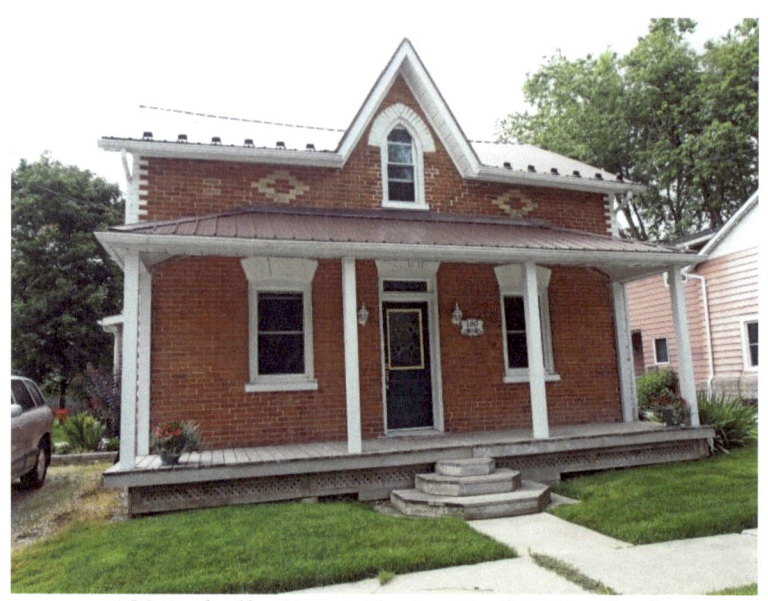

180 Isabella Street East – Gothic Revival

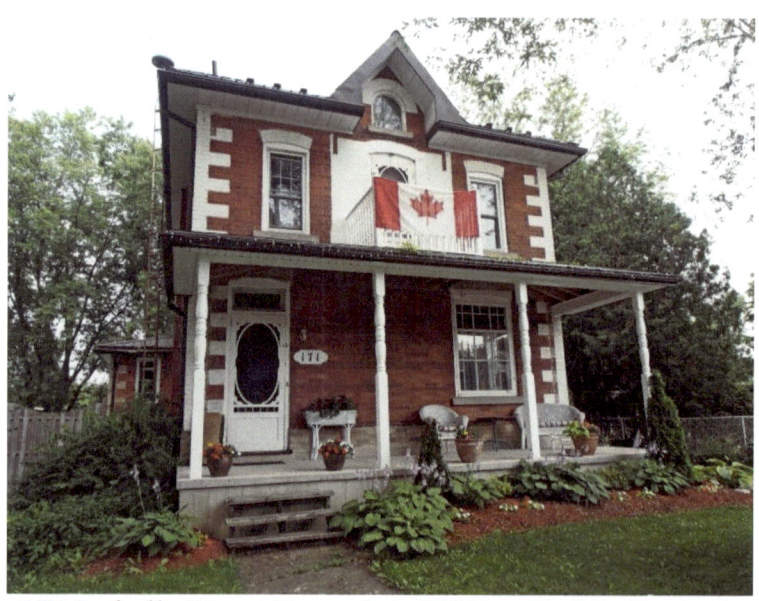

171 Isabella Street East – late 1800s – Gothic Revival,
corner quoins

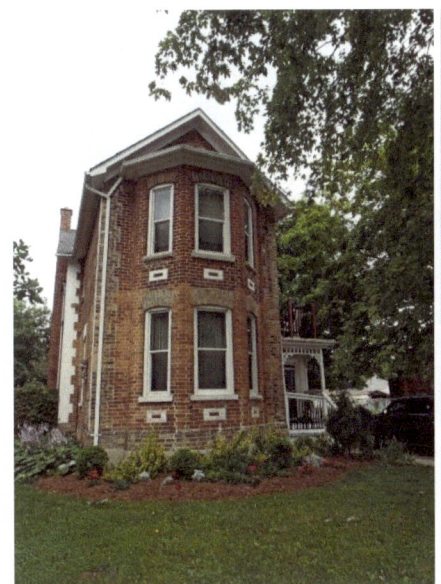

Isabella Street East

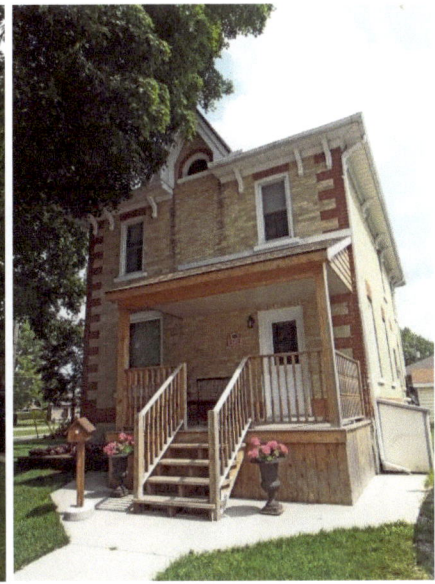

140 Leonard Street

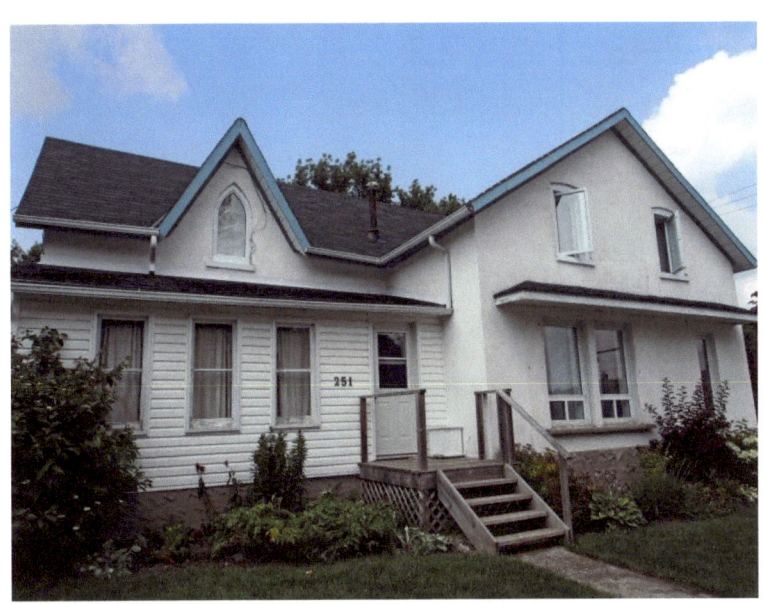

251 Leonard Street – Gothic Revival

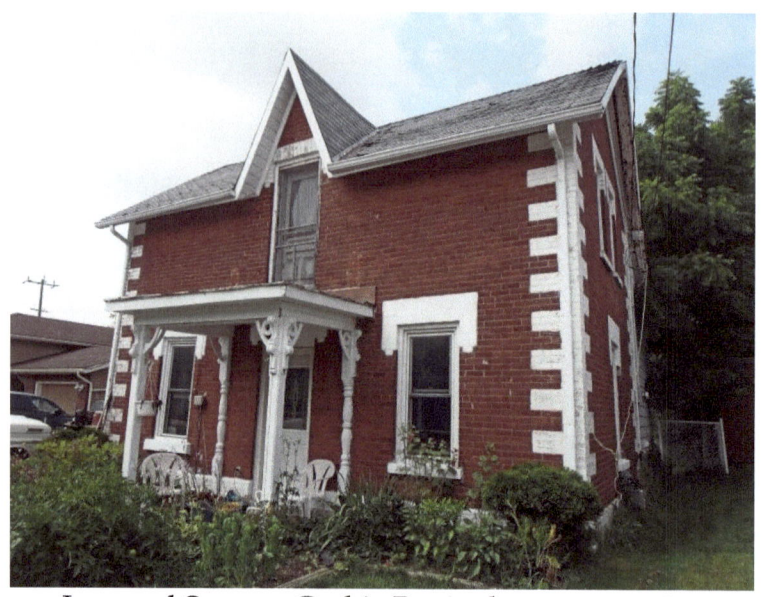

Leonard Street – Gothic Revival, corner quoins

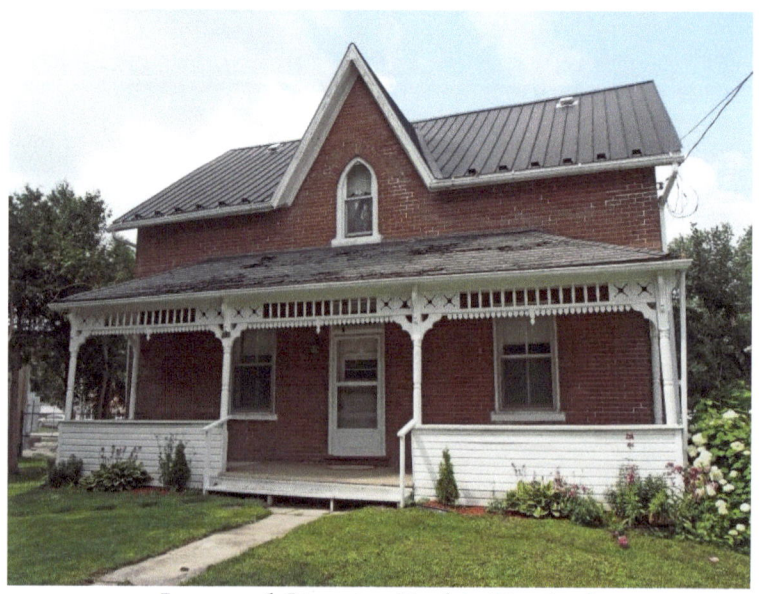

Leonard Street – Gothic Revival

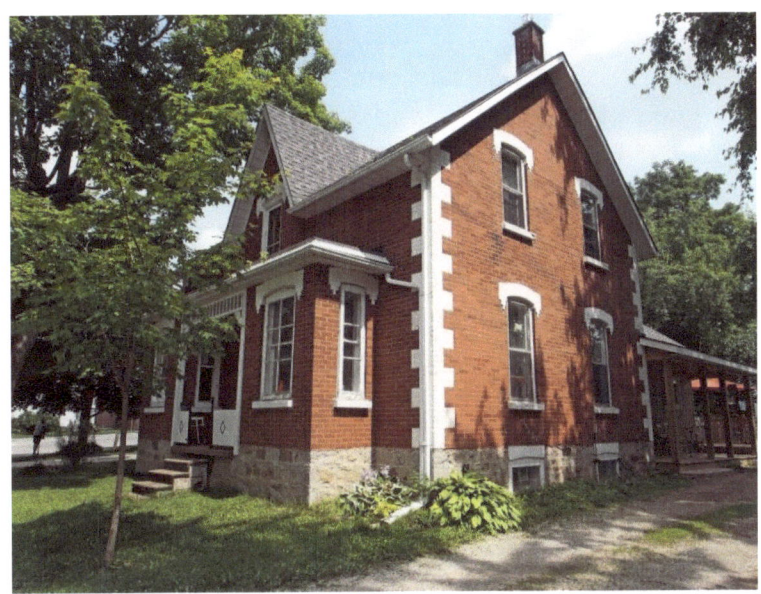

200 Leonard Street – Gothic Revival, corner quoins

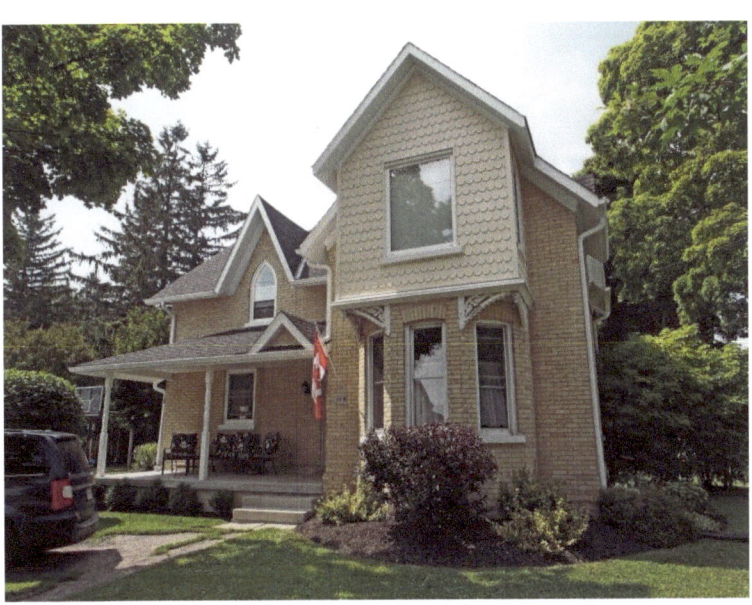

Leonard Street – Gothic Revival

Architectural Terms

Banding: Different materials, colours or textures used in horizontal bands along a wall. Example: 105 Tucker Street, Grace Anglican Church	
Brackets: a decorative or weight-bearing structural element which forms a right angle with one side against a wall and the other under a projecting surface such as an eave or roof. Example: 261 Smith Street	
Buttress: a masonry structure built against or projecting from a wall which serves to support or reinforce the wall. In Canadian architecture, they are sometimes used for decoration. Example: 105 Tucker Street, Grace Anglican Church	
Cobblestone architecture: Refers to the use of cobblestones embedded in mortar as a method for erecting walls on houses and commercial buildings. Example: 121 Isabella Street West	
Cornice: originally the wooden overhang of the roof. With the use of stone, brick, iron and steel, the cornice is any projecting shelf at the top of a ceiling or roof. They can be very decorative. Example: 141 Frederick Street East	
Cornice Return: decorative element on the end of a gable. Example: 131 Frederick Street West	

Dentil Moulding: an even series of rectangles used as ornamental decoration in cornices. Example: downtown	
Dichromatic brickwork: the use of two colours of brick, tile or slate to decorate a façade. Example: 135 Frederick Street West	
Dormer: (French for "sleep") a gable end window that pierces through the plane of a sloping roof surface to create usable space in the top floor or attic of a building by adding headroom. Example: 261 Smith Street	
Entrance: The entrance encompasses the doorway and the inner vestibule or, in residential architecture, the covered porch. Example: Arthur United Church	
Gable: the triangular portion of a wall between the edges of a sloping roof. Example: 111 Frederick Street West	
Hipped Roof: a roof where all sides slope downwards to the walls with no gables. Example: 261 Smith Street	
Lancet Window: a tall, narrow window with a pointed arch at its top. Example: St. Andrew's Presbyterian Church	

Mansard Roof: This style was popularized by Francois Mansart (1598-1666), an accomplished architect of the French Baroque period and especially fashionable during the Second French Empire (1852-1870). This roof is almost flat on the top section, with two slopes on each of its sides with the lower slope at a steeper angle than the upper and having dormer windows. Example: see Page 38	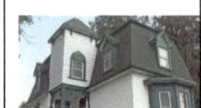
Palladian Window: a large window that is divided into three sections with the centre section larger than the two side sections and usually arched. Example: 291 Smith Street	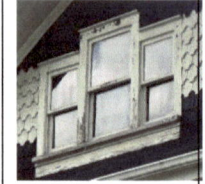
Quoin: masonry blocks at the corner of a wall, often a decorative feature, usually larger or of a different colour than the rest of the wall. Example: 111 Frederick Street West	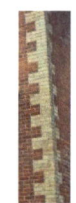
Rose Window: a circular window with ornamental tracery radiating from the centre. Example: Arthur United Church	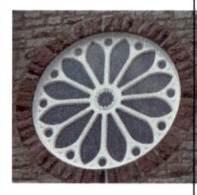

Turret: a small tower that projects from the wall of a building. Example: see Page 39	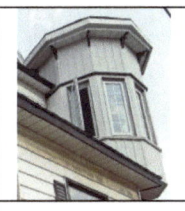
Vergeboard and Finial: also called bargeboards – hang from the projecting end of a roof and are often elaborately carved and ornamented. **Finial:** ornament added to the top of a gable, pinnacle, canopy or spire – a Gothic element. Example: 271 Smith Street	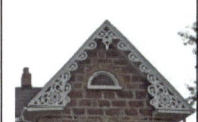
Keystones and Voussoirs: a voussoir is a wedge-shaped element used in building an arch. A keystone is the central stone that locks all the stones into position, allowing the arch to bear weight. A keystone is often enlarged and embellished. Example: 261 Isabella Street	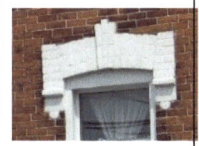

Edwardian, 1900-1930 – This style bridges the ornate and elaborate styles of the Victorian era and the simplified styles of the 20th century. Balanced facades, simple roof lines, dormer windows, large front porches, and smooth brick surfaces are its characteristics. Example: 291 Smith Street	
Gothic Revival, 1830-1890 – These decorative buildings have sharply-pitched gables with highly detailed vergeboards, pointed-arch window openings, and dichromatic brickwork. It is a common style in Ontario. Example: Leonard Street (see Page 50)	
Italianate, 1850-1900 – It has wide-bracketed eaves, belvederes, wrap-around verandahs. Example: 171 Tucker Street	
Second Empire, 1860-1880 – The mansard roof is the most noteworthy feature of this style and is evidence of the French origins. Projecting central towers and one or two-storey bays can also be present. Example: 261 Tucker Street	

www.ingramcontent.com/pod-product-compliance
Lightning Source LLC
Chambersburg PA
CBHW040854180526
45159CB00001B/425